Alexandra Teynor

Visual Object Class Recognition using Local Descriptions

Alexandra Teynor

Visual Object Class Recognition using Local Descriptions

Südwestdeutscher Verlag für Hochschulschriften

Impressum/Imprint (nur für Deutschland/ only for Germany)
Bibliografische Information der Deutschen Nationalbibliothek: Die Deutsche Nationalbibliothek verzeichnet diese Publikation in der Deutschen Nationalbibliografie; detaillierte bibliografische Daten sind im Internet über http://dnb.d-nb.de abrufbar.
Alle in diesem Buch genannten Marken und Produktnamen unterliegen warenzeichen-, marken- oder patentrechtlichem Schutz bzw. sind Warenzeichen oder eingetragene Warenzeichen der jeweiligen Inhaber. Die Wiedergabe von Marken, Produktnamen, Gebrauchsnamen, Handelsnamen, Warenbezeichnungen u.s.w. in diesem Werk berechtigt auch ohne besondere Kennzeichnung nicht zu der Annahme, dass solche Namen im Sinne der Warenzeichen- und Markenschutzgesetzgebung als frei zu betrachten wären und daher von jedermann benutzt werden dürften.

Verlag: Südwestdeutscher Verlag für Hochschulschriften GmbH & Co. KG
Dudweiler Landstr. 99, 66123 Saarbrücken, Deutschland
Telefon +49 681 37 20 271-1, Telefax +49 681 37 20 271-0
Email: info@svh-verlag.de
Zugl.: Freiburg, Albert-Ludwigs-Universität, Dissertation, 2008

Herstellung in Deutschland:
Schaltungsdienst Lange o.H.G., Berlin
Books on Demand GmbH, Norderstedt
Reha GmbH, Saarbrücken
Amazon Distribution GmbH, Leipzig
ISBN: 978-3-8381-0578-9

Imprint (only for USA, GB)
Bibliographic information published by the Deutsche Nationalbibliothek: The Deutsche Nationalbibliothek lists this publication in the Deutsche Nationalbibliografie; detailed bibliographic data are available in the Internet at http://dnb.d-nb.de.
Any brand names and product names mentioned in this book are subject to trademark, brand or patent protection and are trademarks or registered trademarks of their respective holders. The use of brand names, product names, common names, trade names, product descriptions etc. even without a particular marking in this works is in no way to be construed to mean that such names may be regarded as unrestricted in respect of trademark and brand protection legislation and could thus be used by anyone.

Publisher: Südwestdeutscher Verlag für Hochschulschriften GmbH & Co. KG
Dudweiler Landstr. 99, 66123 Saarbrücken, Germany
Phone +49 681 37 20 271-1, Fax +49 681 37 20 271-0
Email: info@svh-verlag.de

Printed in the U.S.A.
Printed in the U.K. by (see last page)
ISBN: 978-3-8381-0578-9

Copyright © 2011 by the author and Südwestdeutscher Verlag für Hochschulschriften GmbH & Co. KG and licensors
All rights reserved. Saarbrücken 2011

Alexandra Teynor

Visual Object Class Recognition using Local Descriptions

Dissertation zur Erlangung des Doktorgrades
der Fakultät für Angewandte Wissenschaften
der Albert-Ludwigs-Universität Freiburg im Breisgau
Dezember 2008

Dekan:	Prof. Dr. Bernard Nebel
Prüfungskommission:	Prof. Dr. Matthias Teschner (Vorsitz)
	Prof. Dr. Wolfram Burgard (Beisitz)
	Prof. Dr.-Ing. Hans Burkhardt (Betreuer)
	Prof. Dr. Thomas Vetter (Gutachter)
Datum der Disputation:	3. Dezember 2008

Deutsche Zusammenfassung

Die vorliegende Arbeit beschäftigt sich mit der Erkennung von Elementen visueller Objektklassen in digitalen Bildern. Diese Aufgabe stellt sich beispielsweise, will man den Inhalt großer Bild- und Videodatenbanken zugänglich machen. Bilder, die bestimmte Objekte enthalten, sollen leicht (wieder-) gefunden werden. Traditionelle Ansätze wie die Verwendung von Schlagwörtern für einzelne Bilder sind nur eingeschränkt tauglich, da sie kostenintensiv, subjektiv und sprachabhängig sind. Ziel ist es daher, Verfahren zu entwickeln, die nur auf den Bilddaten selbst beruhen.

Das grundlegende Prinzip der in dieser Arbeit vorgestellten Methoden ist die Verwendung von lokalen, visuellen Merkmalen, die aus den Bildern extrahiert werden. Die Arbeit besitzt zwei Schwerpunkte: der erste Abschnitt beschäftigt sich mit der Identifikation und der Repräsentation von Objektteilen. Der zweite Abschnitt beleuchtet Methoden, wie die Objektteile miteinander in (örtliche) Verbindung gesetzt werden können, um damit verschiedene Objektklassen zu modellieren. Im Folgenden werden die beiden Schwerpunkte kurz beschrieben.

Identifikation von Teilen

Um Orte für die lokale Merkmalsextraktion zu bestimmen, werden spezielle Detektoren (*interest point detectors*) verwendet, die Punkte mit gewünschten Eigenschaften identifizieren. Welchen Kriterien diese Punkte entsprechen müssen, hängt von der Anwendung ab. Die Analyse einer Vielzahl von Detektoren zeigte, dass eine zu frühe Beschränkung der Art der detektierten Strukturen die Klassifikationsleistung negativ beeinflusst. Der von uns in dieser Arbeit verwendete Loupias-Detektor besitzt diesbezüglich sehr gute Eigenschaften. Er beruht auf einer Waveletanalyse des Signals, liefert in seiner Originalversion jedoch keine Größeninformation. Daher wurde dieser Detektor mit Hilfe eines Skalenselektionsverfahrens erweitert. Mit diesem neuen Detektor konnten hervorragende Ergebnisse bei einer anspruchsvollen Klassifikationsaufgabe von Tierbildern erzielt werden. Der dabei verwendete Datensatz wurde im Rahmen des MUSCLE Network-of-Excellence zusammengestellt.

An den detektierten Stellen im Bild werden verschiedene Merkmale berechnet, welche die lokale Struktur beschreiben. Diese Merkmale werden zur Konstruktion von Teilewörterbüchern verwendet, deren Einträge als Bausteine zur Erstellung von Objektklassenmodellen dienen. In dieser Arbeit konnte gezeigt werden, dass komplizierte, zeitintensive Verfahren, welche die genaue Anordnung der Lernstichproben in Merkmalsräumen berücksichtigen, zur Bestimmung der Prototypteile nicht nötig sind. Vielmehr reicht ein einfaches, sequenzielles Verfahren (*MBSAS-clustering*) aus, um geeignete Teilewörterbücher zu erzeugen. Die Berechnungszeit solcher Wörterbücher konnte von mehreren Tagen auf wenige Stunden reduziert werden.

In herkömmlichen Teilewörterbüchern werden nur visuell ähnliche Strukturen zu Prototypteilen zusammengefasst. Bestimmte, semantisch äquivalente Teile eines Objekts können jedoch sehr unterschiedliche visuelle Ausprägungen haben. Wenn diese von der

Bedeutung her gleichen Teile getrennt behandelt werden, können Einbußen in der Klassifikationsleistung entstehen. In dieser Arbeit wurde ein Verfahren entwickelt, visuell unterschiedliche, aber semantisch ähnliche Teile zu assoziieren. Dies geschieht mit Hilfe eines semantischen Ähnlichkeitsmaßes, das auf örtlichen Auftretensverteilungen beruht. Damit konnte die Klassifikationsleistung eines Nächste-Nachbarn-Klassifikators verbessert sowie die Komplexität einer SVM-Klassifikation (*support vector maschine*) gesenkt werden.

Assoziation von Teilen zur Objektmodellierung

Im zweiten Teil der Arbeit werden verschiedene Verfahren vorgestellt, einzelne Prototypen aus den Teilewörterbüchern zueinander in Verbindung zu setzten. Eine etablierte Methode ist die Verwendung von Teilehistogrammen, welche die Auftretenshäufigkeit bestimmter Teile modellieren. Da bei der Ähnlichkeitsbestimmung der Vergleich der Teilehäufigkeiten für die einzelnen Teile getrennt erfolgt, ist eine semantische Zusammenfassung visuell unterschiedlicher Teile, wie im ersten Teil gezeigt, notwendig.

Die Auswertung der relativen Position von Paaren lokaler Teile führt zu sogenannten *cluster co-occurrence* Matrizen. Diese Matrizen wurden als Merkmale zur Klassifikation von Röntgenaufnahmen eingesetzt. Damit konnten im „ImageCLEF medical image annotation" Wettbewerb in den Jahren 2006 und 2007 ausgezeichnete Ergebnisse erzielt werden.

Mit Hilfe lokaler Teile kann neben der Klassifikation auch die exakte Position eines Objektes im Bild ermittelt werden. Im Rahmen dieser Arbeit wurde eine Methode entwickelt, die nicht nur die Lage und Größe eines Objekts, sondern auch dessen Orientierung erkennt. Diese beruht auf einem Hough-Mehrheitsverfahren und beachtet die Orientierung der einzelnen Detektionen im Bild.

Bei Verfahren zur Bestimmung der wahrscheinlichen Lageparameter eines Objekts liegt die Annahme zugrunde, dass ein Objekt der Klasse im Bild vorhanden ist. Ob dies tatsächlich der Fall ist, wird nicht überprüft. Daher wird in dieser Arbeit vorgeschlagen, die Positionsparameterbestimmung mit der Erzeugung von lokalen Teilehistogrammen zu kombinieren, um damit eine Klassifikation von Bildern zu ermöglichen. Von Regionen mit einer hohen Auftretenswahrscheinlichkeit für das Objekt werden lokale Histogramme berechnet. Um die Klassifikationssicherheit von herkömmlichen regionenbasierten Histogrammen zu steigern, wurden SCP (*spatially coherent parts*) Histogramme entwickelt. Diese bestehen nur aus den Teilen, die für eine bestimmte Parameterkombination eines Objektes gestimmt haben. Dadurch entstehen Vorteile bei teilweise verdeckten Objekten sowie Objekten, durch die der Hintergrund durchscheint. Ein Test der neuen Verfahren auf einer schwierigen Fahrraddatenbank hat deren klare Überlegenheit gegenüber globalen Histogrammansätzen gezeigt.

Der letzte Abschnitt der Arbeit zeigt mögliche Erweiterungen der vorgestellten Systeme auf, welche insbesondere in der Entwicklung von dreidimensionalen Modellen sowie im automatischen Lernen aus Videodaten zu sehen sind.

Abstract

This work is concerned with the recognition of visual object class members in digital images. The fundamental principle of all methods employed in this work is the use of local, visual features extracted from the images. There are two emphases: the first half of the work deals with the identification and the representation of the local object parts, the second half analyzes and proposes methods how to relate the object parts in order to build object class models. In the following, we give a short overview about the two emphases:

Determining parts

In order to identify locations for feature extraction, *interest point detectors* are used. Depending on the precise type of the detector, different kinds of structures can be discovered. We evaluated the properties of several detectors and could show that restricting the type of structure to be found too early can be harmful for the recognition performance. In this respect, the wavelet-based Loupias detector used in this work possesses beneficial properties. However, in its original version, it does not provide any scale information. For this reason, we extended the Loupias detector by a Laplacian scale selection mechanism. we could obtain superior results using this extended detector in a challenging animal classification task proposed by the MUSCLE Network-of-Excellence.

From the regions discovered by the individual interest point detectors, visual features are calculated. These local descriptions of the structures under consideration can be used to construct *part dictionaries* or *visual codebooks*. The individual entries of these dictionaries serve as building blocks for object class models. In this work, we analyzed different state-of-the art methods for building visual codebooks. We were able to show that difficult, time-consuming algorithms, that try to recover the precise layout of the samples in feature space are not necessary. A simple sequential algorithm (*MBSAS-clustering*) is sufficient to construct high quality codebooks. In this way, we were able to reduce the time for constructing visual codebooks from several days to few hours.

The visual codebooks contain a variety of different visual parts. Certain structures might have a common semantic meaning, but look considerably different. Treating these semantically related, but visually different entities separately can spoil the recognition performance. This work presents a method how these semantically related parts can be associated by comparing their object reference point distributions. Using semantically recombined features leads to improved recognition performance for nearest neighbor classifiers and enhanced speed for SVM based classification.

Relating parts

The second focus of this work is on methods how to combine the prototype parts to create object class models. An established way is to just consider the occurrence frequencies of the individual structures. A more sophisticated technique is to examine the pairwise relationship of the parts. This lead to the development of *cluster co-occurrence matrices*. These features were used for the classification of radiograph images in the ImageCLEF medical image annotation challenge. Superior results could be achieved for the 2006 and 2007 competitions.

The local parts can also be used to recover the positional parameters of an object. In this work, we present a method that is not only capable of estimating the location and the scale of an object, but also its orientation. This is achieved by using a Hough-like voting scheme and object reference point distributions as well as the orientation of the local detections in the image.

Methods to identify probable object parameters already assume that the object is indeed present in an image, but it can not be inferred whether this is true. We propose to combine an object parameter estimation stage and the creation of local histograms from the estimated object region to enable object classification. To improve the capabilities of the traditional regional histograms, we have developed histograms of *spatially coherent parts* (SCP). These are histograms only from parts that agree on a specific object parameter configuration. Tests on a challenging bicycle database have shown the superiority of the approach compared to a global bag-of-features approach.

The last part of this work offers an outlook to possible extensions of our systems, in particular the construction of three dimensional models and the development of learning algorithms using video data.

Acknowledgment

The successful completion of this work would not have been possible without the help of other people.

First, I would like to thank Prof. Dr.-Ing. Hans Burkhardt for giving me the opportunity to work in his group. He provided an excellently equipped environment and gave me the freedom to pursue independent research in the very interesting field of visual object class recognition.

I would also like to thank Prof. Dr. Thomas Vetter for his interest in my work and for agreeing to be the co-examiner of this thesis. The examination committee was completed by Prof. Dr. Matthias Teschner and Prof. Dr. Wolfram Burgard, whom I would like to thank for taking on this responsibility.

I would especially like to thank all my colleagues from the pattern recognition and image processing group. In particular, I want to mention some people who directly influenced the progress of my work through discussions, hints or proofreading of manuscripts: Bernard Haasdonk especially helped me at the beginning of my work and brought me on track. Lokesh Setia and Alaa Halawani shared similar scientific goals, and thus we had many fruitful discussions. Olaf Ronneberger always had a pool of remarks and tried to teach me how to sell washing powder. Thorsten Schmidt is a programming compendium and Marco Reisert has a quite formal view on things – both characteristics helped this work. I would also like to thank my colleagues Robert Bensch, Nikos Canterakis, Mario Emmenlauer, Janis Fehr, Dimitris Katsoulas, Margret Keuper, Klaus-Dieter Peschke, Janina Schulz, Henrik Skibbe, Maja Temerinac and Qing Wang for making LMB a very pleasant place to work. A kind thank-you also goes to Esa Rahtu from the university of Oulu, Finland, with whom I had the chance to work during his stay at our chair.

I would also like to thank all my students who conducted their student research theses, diploma or master theses under my guidance. They contributed various insights.

Cynthia Findlay and Stefan Teister helped this work by relieving me of administrative and technical burdens and thus giving me more time to focus on scientific issues. Thank you!

And there is another group of people, who did not contribute to this work in a strictly scientific way, but were still important: very sincere thanks go to all my friends in Freiburg, Friedberg and everywhere else, for all the great times spent outside the academic world.

Last but not least, I would like to thank my family. Stefan Jansen stopped me from getting lost in my office, provided me with excellent music and also contributed to this thesis by casting a mathematical eye on the formulas. My parents Isolde and Günter raised me in a way that made me curious about this world and encouraged me to explore it. My brother Oliver is not just a brother, but also a friend. I am deeply grateful for all their love, encouragement and constant support.

Freiburg, January 2009 *Alexandra Teynor*

„Ich stehe am Fenster und sehe ein Haus, Bäume, Himmel. Und könnte nun, aus theoretischen Gründen, abzuzählen versuchen und sagen: da sind ... 327 Helligkeiten (und Farbtöne). (Habe ich „327"? Nein; Himmel, Haus, Bäume; [...])"

(Wertheimer, 1923)

Contents

1	**Introduction**	**1**
1.1	Problem Statement	3
1.2	Object Class Recognition using Local Descriptions	6
1.3	Basic Principles and Organization of the Thesis	8
1.4	Contribution of this Thesis	10
I	**Determining Parts**	**11**
2	**Interest Point Detection**	**13**
2.1	State-of-the-Art	14
	2.1.1 Point Detectors	15
	2.1.2 Scale Selection Methods	21
	2.1.3 Region Detectors	25
2.2	Extension of the Wavelet Based Interest Point Detector	27
2.3	Experimental Evaluation	29
	2.3.1 Repeatability and Accuracy	29
	2.3.2 Structure Variety	32
	2.3.3 Object Classification	37
2.4	Discussion	39
3	**Local Features**	**41**
3.1	Basic Notion	41
3.2	Feature Distributions	43
3.3	Basic Feature Types	45
	3.3.1 Color Features	46
	3.3.2 Texture Features	46
	3.3.3 Shape Features	49
3.4	Combining Features	51
3.5	Discussion	52
4	**Visual Codebooks**	**53**
4.1	Related Work	54
4.2	Sequential Clustering	55
	4.2.1 Clustering Algorithm	55

ix

Contents

		4.2.2	Determining the Similarity Threshold	56
	4.3	Experimental Evaluation		59
		4.3.1	Codebook Statistics	60
		4.3.2	Classification Results	60
		4.3.3	Run-times	65
	4.4	Discussion		66

5 Semantic Codebooks   67
   5.1   Related Work 68
   5.2   Semantic Recombination 68
   5.3   Experimental Evaluation 71
   5.4   Discussion 75

II   Relating Parts   77

6   General Principles for Relating Parts   79

7   Bag-of-Features Model   81
   7.1   Parzen Window Density Estimation 81
   7.2   Object Representation 83

8   Co-occurrence of Parts   85
   8.1   Related Work 85
   8.2   Cluster Co-occurrence Matrices 85
   8.3   Experimental Evaluation 87
   8.4   Discussion 88

9   Part Relations to a Reference Point   91

	9.1	Identification of Object Parameters		91
		9.1.1	Related Work	91
		9.1.2	Proposed Method	93
		9.1.3	Experimental Results	100
		9.1.4	Discussion	106
	9.2	Geometrically Stable Object Parts		107
	9.3	Object Classification		111
		9.3.1	Related Work	112
		9.3.2	Regional Part Histograms	112
		9.3.3	Histograms of Spatially Coherent Parts	113
		9.3.4	Experimental Evaluation	114
		9.3.5	Discussion	116

10   Summary and Conclusion   121
   10.1   Identifying and Representing Parts 121

	10.2 Creating Object Class Models by Relating Parts	122
	10.3 Perspectives	124
A	**Notation**	**125**
B	**Abbreviations**	**129**
C	**Performance Measures**	**131**
	Bibliography	**134**

1 Introduction

Today, a huge amount of digital photographs exists on private computers, on the web or in professional media archives, and the mass will continue to grow. Current image databases of publishing companies already reach many thousands of terabytes of data.

Retrieving images from these large databases is difficult. Think about your own holiday picture collection: linear search through the archives is hardly feasible on home desktop computers. Manual annotation of images to enable text retrieval techniques is no general solution either. It is very laborious and thus cost intensive. Moreover, annotation by key words is subjective, since visual content tends to be interpreted in different ways by humans. Other drawbacks are the language dependency of the key words, the key word ambiguities, equivalent key words, the possibility of spelling mistakes or simply the use of wrong key words. Professional image classification schemes as used for physical image archives like the ICONCLASS (van de Waal, 1954) scheme try to overcome some of these difficulties by formalizing the image description, however, they are difficult to handle by laymen.

We need automatic techniques based on the image content in order to cope with the sheer amount of data. Research dealing with this topic is comprised under the label *Content Based Image Retrieval* (CBIR). Rather than dealing with a single problem, CBIR involves many different tasks. One of the first challenges met was the search for *similar* images, where the notion of similar was mainly defined from a color, texture and sometimes shape point of view. The images were treated more or less globally, later also local considerations came into play. This problem was heavily investigated in the 1990s and early 2000s, and work on this topic is still in progress. In a traditional CBIR system, one or more example images are used as input, for which then similar images are retrieved from the database. They are displayed to the user in the order of their relevance. This search method is known as *query-by-example* paradigm.

A more general problem is the search for specific objects. Users are interested in finding semantic entities in images like people, cars or animals rather than just finding images with a similar color distribution. The search for objects can be divided into two main cases: the first one is the detection of the very same physical object in different images, the other one is the recognition of members of an object class. In order to be recognized by their appearance, the objects have to share some visual characteristics.

1 Introduction

Eakins and Graham (1999) proposed a classification scheme for different CBIR query types consisting of three levels of increasing complexity. The partition of the query types was made as follows:

Level 1: Search by primitive features Images are retrieved by basic features like color, texture, shape, spatial layout or combinations of these. Most traditional image retrieval systems, as e.g. QBIC (Flickner et al., 1995), SIMBA (Siggelkow et al., 2001), VIPER/GIFT (Müller, 2001), or FIRE (Deselaers et al., 2004) work on this level. All information necessary for relevance assessment can be acquired from the images themselves.

Level 2: Search by derived/logical features There are two subtasks falling into this category:

1. *Retrieval of objects of a given type*
   The search for members of a visual object class belongs into this category. In current research, the object classes to be searched for are rather narrow, however also more general classes like, e.g., "flowers" or "animals" can be considered.

2. *Retrieval of individual objects or persons*
   Here, exactly the same instance of an object or person should be retrieved. Even if this task sounds more difficult, since, e.g., not only any car, but a special car is searched for, this is an easier task for a computer, since less variety in its appearance has to be taken into account.

Besides the pure image content, additional knowledge is necessary for the retrieval of correct images, e.g. that a certain structure has been given a specific name or that a visual object class has certain properties.

Level 3: Search by abstract features In this category, the meaning and purpose of images should be evaluated, so high level reasoning is necessary. To our knowledge, currently no systems are working at this level. An exception might a system by Corridoni et al. (1998), that interprets the meaning of the prevalent colors in an image. Again, two cases can be distinguished:

1. *Retrieval of named events or types of activity*
   Images associated to a football match or an event like, e.g., the "Olympics" fall into this category. The visual variety of such images is enormous, so learning is difficult.

2. *Retrieval of pictures with emotional or religious significance*
   This class comprises images showing contents like love, hate or salvation. The mood of the images has to be judged, something that even humans do not easily agree on. This stage of image retrieval is not likely to be solved by machines in the near future.

In this thesis, we deal with queries at level two, in particular with "retrieval of objects of a given type". In the following, we want to clarify our notion of the terms *object* and *visual object class*.

Object: *"something material that may be perceived by the senses"* (Merriam-Webster, 2003)
In our work, we only deal with physical objects that can be counted. e.g., we would not consider "snow" an object, but a "snow crystal". The objects should also have limited extents, so that they can be captured by images.

Visual object class: *"a collection of objects that share some visual characteristics"*
Examples for visual classes are "cars", "faces" or "motorbikes", since they all have certain visual properties in common. The object class "tools" would not fall into this category, since tools might look completely different, and the grouping is made from a functional point of view.

1.1 Problem Statement

A typical example for a CBIR query at level two in the above mentioned scheme is whether and possibly where a bicycle is shown in a photograph. This question sounds easy, since for humans this is a simple task. Even toddlers are already able to recognize many object categories. However, for a computer, the recognition of object class members is a very difficult problem. Why is this? In the following, we attempt to shed some light on this issue.

Intra class variability
Objects of the same visual class might still have a great variability in appearance and layout of the individual parts. Even if we have a very narrow object category, e.g. "bicycle", and they are all viewed from the same perspective, e.g., the side, they can look rather different in detail (see figure 1.1).

Figure 1.1: Object variability for the side view of the class bicycle.

3D objects in 2D images

In the real world, we deal with 3D objects. When they are projected onto a 2D image, information is lost, since not all views of the object can be captured at the same time. A bicycle looks very different seen from different sides, as can be seen in figure 1.2. We humans have no difficulty in recognizing these objects even so, since we know all views and how they are related. We have a 3D model of the object class in mind. A general object recognition system would also require this information. One could either supply it with a full 3D model, as e.g., Ponce et al. (2004); Romdhani and Vetter (2007), or with a sufficient number of 2D model views that are set into relation, as e.g., Thomas et al. (2006). A more restrictive but widely adopted approach is to limit the search to a specific view, e.g. exclusively side views of cars or frontal views of faces (Fergus et al., 2003).

To make things more tractable, one often assumes planar objects, or at least planar object parts. If we only consider small regions on the surface of a smooth object, this is approximately true. The parts can undergo a variety of transformations between images. To further simplify things, we assume infinite cameras and thus transformations only up to affinity, since they are more easy to handle mathematically. We then can express the relationship of the coordinates of a point $\mathbf{x} = (x, y)^\top \in \mathbb{R}^2$ in an image and the transformed coordinates $\mathbf{x}'$ in another image by

$$\mathbf{x}' = \mathbf{T}\mathbf{x} + \mathbf{t}, \tag{1.1}$$

where the $\mathbf{t} \in \mathbb{R}^2$ denotes the translation and the properties of the real matrix $\mathbf{T} \in \mathbb{R}^{2 \times 2}$ describe the type of the transformation:

$$\begin{aligned}
\mathbf{T} &= \mathbb{1}_2 & &\textbf{translation,} \\
\mathbf{T}^\top \mathbf{T} &= \mathbb{1}_2 & &\textbf{congruence transformation,} \\
\mathbf{T}^\top \mathbf{T} &= \kappa \mathbb{1}_2 & &\textbf{similarity transformation } (\kappa \in \mathbb{R} \setminus \{0\}), \\
\det(\mathbf{T}) &\neq 0 & &\textbf{affine transformation.}
\end{aligned}$$

The n-dimensional identity matrix is denoted by $\mathbb{1}_n$. These geometric distortions make a direct comparison of images of even the same object difficult, since the precise transformation parameters are typically unknown.

Occlusions

In many real world photographs, the object is only partially visible, since it is occluded to some extent, or some parts of the object stretch beyond the image border.

Recording procedure

The recording process can also introduce errors. These can be, e.g., noise, quantization errors, discretization errors, image blur, but also compression artefacts.

1.1 Problem Statement

Figure 1.2: A specific object (here my bike) from different views.

Illumination changes
Objects captured in the real world might be illuminated very differently. We have to deal with additive (the basic brightness is higher), multiplicative (higher contrast) and non-linear (light source at a different direction) illumination changes.

Non rigid transformations of the object itself
Some object classes are composed of articulated parts, e.g., humans, which makes recognition according to the shape difficult. Other objects have a soft structure with no specific outline, e.g., clouds or cuddly toys. Even if we have a comparatively well defined object class like pollen grains, methods also taking into account the local deformations of the objects can improve classification performance (Ronneberger et al., 2007).

Ratio image area to object area
The object might only cover a small part of the image, while background clutter or other objects dominate the scene. This makes the recognition of these small objects very difficult, especially if we have no a priori information about the scale of the object.

Inadequacies of the mathematical model
When modelling is an issue, we usually have to make simplifying assumptions about some conditions, in order to keep the problem computationally feasible. In reality however, we might have different conditions, e.g., non-linearities, non-planarities or statistical dependencies where we assumed none.

1 Introduction

Figure 1.3: Images representing a more semantic notion of the class bicycles.

Semantic notion

Images depicting the same object class might look rather different. As human beings, we always have a semantic interpretation of what we see. This fact is known from CBIR and called the "semantic gap". In Santini et al. (2000, p. 1353), it is defined as:

"The semantic gap is the lack of coincidence between the information that one can extract from the visual data and the interpretation that the same data have for a user in a given situation."

How different images with the same semantic interpretation (here a bicycle) might look can be seen in figure 1.3. Not only the views and display details are different, but also the styles in which the images are made. Here we would rather deal with a semantic than with a visual object class.

As can be seen from the collection of problems above, a variety of things has to be considered when the recognition of visual object class members should be successful. In current systems, typically only certain aspects are addressed. Many databases used for evaluation, e.g. the Caltech databases, make assumptions about the location, size and/or orientation of the objects. This is necessary in order to better understand the effects of the algorithms. The main simplification made in this work is that the different views of an object are modelled separately. Chapter 10 discusses some ideas how the different views can be related by a three dimensional object class model.

1.2 Object Class Recognition using Local Descriptions

A very promising way to achieve visual object class recognition is to use local information extracted at distinguished points or areas in an image. Such methods have shown to have benefits over global methods: they are capable of modelling the variability in object appearance as well as shape and can cope with occlusions. In this thesis, we adopt this principle and further develop it.

Methods based on local information are termed differently in literature. The most common notion is *patch based* (e.g. Teynor et al., 2006), however also the term *fragment based* (Ullman et al., 2001), and *part based* (Fischler and Elschlager, 1973) have been used. The first two terms are typically related to primitive extracts acquired from an image, where as the term *part based* is mainly related to more semantic entities, e.g., the arms, the legs, the body or the head for a human being.

The use of local information has many advantages. We summarize them in the following:

Reduction of the amount of data to be processed
Typically, the number of points where local information is extracted is significantly less than the number of pixels in the image. The precise position and scale where features are extracted from can be determined by a variety of different methods. Chapter 2 deals with this in more detail.

Avoidance of segmentation
The objects to be recognized do not have to be segmented prior to recognition, which is a difficult, mathematically ill posed problem.

Robustness to background clutter
Information from the object and the background can be described by different local descriptors. So the description of most object patches is not affected by the background clutter. The classification procedure ideally only considers parts that have a strong indication for the object itself. Information from the background can be used as contextual information or ignored altogether.

Robustness to occlusion
In many real world scenes, objects to be recognized are partially occluded. Global methods that require, e.g., the outline of an object, fail at this point. Patch based approaches have shown to cope well, since the local information acquired at the visible part of an object is not affected by other, occluded parts.

Robustness to variability in object shape
When dealing with visual object classes, we have to cope with variability in shape. When using local information, we detach shape and appearance information and can model them separately. This technique was already proposed by Fischler and Elschlager (1973).

Biological motivation
Whenever a human looks at an image, not all parts are scanned with the same intensity. The eyes perform a number of saccades (fast movements of both eyes in the same direction) and fixations of a scene. The saccades are that fast, that the eye is essentially blind at this time, the transmission of visual information is performed at the fixation times (Rodieck, 1998). So human perception is inherently based on local representations. Although the strength of computers lies in different areas than humans, they might still benefit from efficient mechanisms that have proven to be successful in biological systems.

On the other hand, the use of purely local information also has some disadvantages:

Miss of relevant parts or structures of the image
When using interest point or covariant region detectors, there is always the danger that relevant parts of the object are missed. Later stages in the recognition chain that rely on the detection of these parts might be affected.

Loss of spatial coherence of the parts
If the origin of the local features is discarded as, e.g., in the bag-of-features approaches (see section 7), we lose information. Some parts might only be discriminative within a geometric configuration. Part II deals with techniques how to set parts into relation.

These disadvantages have to be attenuated in order to achieve superior performance. This work offers some solutions.

1.3 Basic Principles and Organization of the Thesis

The main parts of our recognition system are depicted in figure 1.4. The individual stages follow the common pattern recognition scheme, where feature extraction and classification are modelled separately. The chapters of this thesis are arranged in a way consistent to the tasks necessary to build a successful system. In particular, we have divided the work into two main parts: part I deals with the acquisition and the representation of the local structures, part II is concerned with relating the individual parts and building a final object model, which can be used for classification and localization. In the following, we describe the major components of our object recognition system, and indicate their respective treatment in this work.

Identification of the location for feature extraction
Since our premise is to use local information, we first have to determine where the local information should be extracted from the images. Since the calculation of local features at all points in an image is typically too costly, more sophisticated techniques identify different kinds of *interest points*. Chapter 2 covers this issue in detail.

Extraction of local features
A variety of features can be extracted from the local areas detected. Ideally, they are invariant to image transformations, robust against illumination changes as well as noise and capture the properties of the area they are extracted from well. Chapter 3 describes the local feature extraction methods used in this work.

Creation of part dictionaries
In order to simplify the model construction, part dictionaries or visual codebooks are used. They are typically learned from local observations extracted from training images. Chapter 4 is concerned with a particularly fast and simple scheme for the construction of visual codebooks and chapter 5 shows how semantic codebooks can be established.

1.3 Basic Principles and Organization of the Thesis

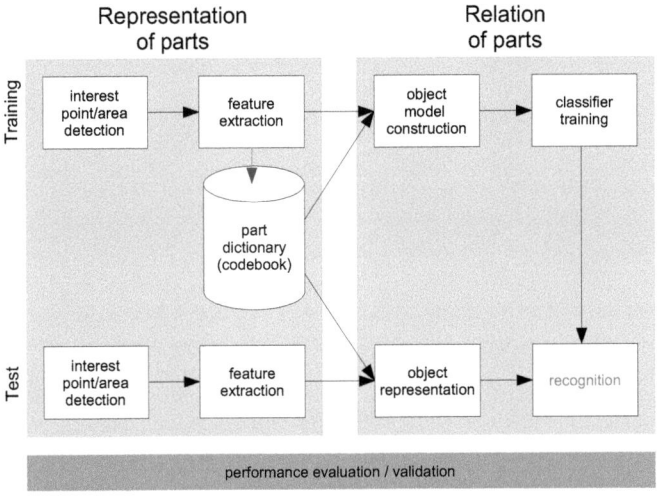

Figure 1.4: General scheme of our object recognition approach.

Model construction and object representation

To describe the object class, we have to learn what is characteristic for it. The local parts that were acquired as described in part I of this work have to be set into relation. Chapters 6 to 9 in part II deal with methods for building object models.

Classification

Based on the object representations, classifiers can be trained. In this work, mainly two established classifiers are used, the simple nearest neighbor classifier for baseline tests and the powerful Support Vector Machine (Schölkopf and Smola, 2001). New images presented to the system for classification typically undergo the same interest point and feature extraction procedure as the training images, and an object representation according to the proposed model is created. Classification and detection experiments are applied in all chapters of this thesis, to evaluate the performance of our algorithms and to verify the hypotheses established.

Validation/Tests

In order to judge the quality of different approaches, they must be evaluated. We used a variety of benchmarks and reference databases. Measures to compare the results are described in appendix C.

1 Introduction

In order to maintain the chapters as self contained as possible, the current state of the art and the related work is directly described in the respective chapters. In appendix A the mathematical notation is described and in appendix B, all abbreviations used are listed.

1.4 Contribution of this Thesis

In the course of this work, we investigated several aspects of object classification using local information. We could contribute findings concerning the following issues:

- Systematic study of properties of patch based approaches for the recognition of visual object classes. First results were published in Teynor et al. (2006), and insights gained during this work were presented in an overview article (Halawani et al., 2006).
- Study of the functionality and suitability of different interest point detectors for object class recognition. In the course of this work, the Loupias interest point detector was extended to provide scale information. This work is presented in section 2.2 and evaluated in section 2.3. The results are published in Teynor and Burkhardt (2008b).
- Development of a fast, sequential clustering scheme to obtain prototype parts for object classification from local information, initially presented in Teynor and Burkhardt (2007a).
- Development of a semantic grouping method for visual parts. The details are covered in chapter 5 and the essential findings were published in Teynor and Burkhardt (2008a).
- Contributions to the development of cluster co-occurrence features for medical image annotation, initially presented in Setia et al. (2006a). A detailed article describing the features can be found in Setia et al. (2008).
- Development of a method to detect the location, scale and in particular the orientation of visual object class members, published in Teynor and Burkhardt (2007b).
- Identification of geometrically stable object parts for voting based parameter estimation methods, covered in detail in section 9.2.
- Coupling of object parameter estimation and regional histogram creation for image classification. In this context, we developed histograms of spatially coherent parts, i.e. a representation of objects based only on parts that agree on a certain object position. Details can be found in section 9.3.3.

Part I
Determining Parts

2 Interest Point Detection

In order to use local representations for recognition, we first have to decide at which locations in an image local features should be extracted. A variety of methods have been proposed and used. Simple techniques range from exhaustive sampling (e.g. Lazebnik et al., 2006), over grid points (e.g. Deselaers et al., 2005) to random locations (e.g. Siggelkow and Schael, 1999; Maree et al., 2005). A more sophisticated technique is the use of *interest points*. The exact meaning of the term interest point differs from author to author. So Agarwal and Roth (2002) describe them to be *"points that have high information content in terms of the local change in signal"*, where Schmid and Mohr (1997) characterizes them to be *"points where a signal changes two-dimensionally"*. (Lowe, 2004) uses the word *key point*. Other authors, as e.g. Loupias et al. (2000) or Kadir et al. (2004), use the term *salient points* and again have their own definition. The basic objective is always the same though: to find certain, preferably mathematically well-defined locations in images that carry beneficial information for the specific task at hand. These locations should be stable under varying image degradations and transformations.

The benefit of using interest points is to reduce the information to be processed at further stages in the recognition chain and at the same time to focus the attention of the system to specific structures.

The typical notion of interest point is generic. Points of interest might be edges, corners, blob-like entities or any other structures. Of course, a specific kind of structure might be more suitable for certain types of objects, e.g., edge-like structures are useful for describing artificial objects. The selection of discriminative structures for a specific class is typically made at a later stage, based on the pool of possible structures provided by the respective detector. In this way, interest points can be shared between different members of structurally different object classes, and do not have to be recomputed for every individual class. As always, some kind of trade off has to be made. When we restrict ourselves to only consider a very specific type of image structure, we will have few detections, thus gain speed because only little local information has to be processed. But we are also in danger of missing relevant object information. So when building a general object recognition system, the type of structure to be considered should not be restricted too early. This can, e.g., be achieved by running several, complementary detectors or by selecting detectors that provide a variety of structures.

In the following, we review the current state-of-the-art for interest point detection in the context of visual object classification. Based on techniques we found useful, we extend the wavelet-based interest point detector by Loupias and Sebe (1999) in section 2.2 to provide scale information. This novel detector is evaluated together with standard detectors in section 2.3.

2.1 State-of-the-Art

Interest point detection has a long tradition in computer vision for finding point correspondences to reconstruct 3D scenes from 2D views. Many different ways how to obtain interest points have been described. Typically, intensity based methods are applied. They directly use the change in brightness of the image pixels. Here, the Moravec detector (Moravec, 1977) is one of the first to mention. Other techniques are contour based methods or methods based on parametric models, although used less frequently for object class recognition. As the name suggests, contour based methods rely on extracted contours and look for changes in curvature, maxima in curvature or inflexion points. Methods based on parametric models apply minimization methods to, e.g., determine the angle of an L-corner (Rohr, 1992). A detailed overview of classic interest point detection techniques can be found in Schmid et al. (2000).

Traditionally, only gray-scale images are used for interest point detection. In the mean time, work considering color information has been presented by Gouet and Boujemaa (2002) and van de Weijer and Schmid (2006).

The term interest point does not imply any extent, however, features are typically extracted from an area around an interest point. One possibility is to compute the features from a fixed size box or circle around the point. This immediately rises the question of scale, since objects might occur at different scales in images. The brute force solution is to extract features at many different scales. A more elegant method is to use automatic scale selection mechanisms. Some detectors also consider affine distortions, they provide elliptical regions (Kadir et al., 2004; Mikolajczyk and Schmid, 2002) or parallelograms (Tuytelaars and Van Gool, 2000).

For object class recognition, not only regions with change in the image signal might carry beneficial information, but also homogeneous regions. Thus some detectors search for regions with similar properties, like homogeneous color or a specific texture. The MSER detector (Maximally Stable Extremal Regions by Matas et al. (2002)) or the IBR detector (Intensity Based Regions by Tuytelaars and Van Gool (2004)) are examples for that. In their cases, the identified regions might have any form and are not restricted to geometric primitives like circles.

In order to adumbrate the variety of possibilities where to extract local features for object class recognition, we list some techniques:

1. **Naive approaches**
    - Dense sampling (Lazebnik et al., 2006)
    - Random points (Siggelkow and Schael, 1999; Maree et al., 2005)
    - Sparse or dense grid (Deselaers et al., 2005; Lazebnik et al., 2006)
    - Gradient magnitude above a threshold (Mikolajczyk et al., 2003)
2. **Point detectors**
    - Moravec detector (Moravec, 1977)
    - Harris corner detector (Harris and Stephens, 1988)
    - Canny edge detector (Canny, 1986)

2.1 State-of-the-Art

- Förstner interest point detector (Förstner and Gülch, 1987)
- Symmetry based interest point detectors (Loy and Zelinsky, 2003; Donner et al., 2007)
- Wavelet based salient point detector (Loupias et al., 2000)

3. **Region detectors**
   - Harris-Laplace/Harris-Affine detector (Mikolajczyk and Schmid, 2002)
   - Hessian-Laplace/Hessian-Affine detector (Mikolajczyk and Schmid, 2002)
   - MSER (Maximally Stable Extremal Regions) detector (Matas et al., 2002)
   - Laplacian of Gaussian (LoG) detector (Lindeberg, 1998)
   - Difference of Gaussian (DoG) detector (Lowe, 2004)
   - SURF detector (Bay et al., 2006)
   - Intensity Based Regions (IBR) detector (Tuytelaars and Van Gool, 2004)
   - Edge Based Regions (EBR) detector (Tuytelaars and Van Gool, 2004)
   - Kadir & Bradey Salient regions detector (Kadir et al., 2004)

There exist a variety of evaluation papers that try to judge the quality of different detectors, e.g. Schmid et al. (2000); Sebe et al. (2002); Mikolajczyk and Schmid (2004) or Mikolajczyk et al. (2005b). The evaluation criteria are mainly repeatability (robustness against varying imaging conditions like viewpoint, scale, illumination changes) and information content. Mikolajczyk et al. (2005a) evaluated interest point detectors (and features) also in the context of object class recognition, and some of the tests proposed there were adopted for our evaluation in section 2.3.

In the following, we review some basic interest point detection techniques. This is done to provide some insight into their operation principles and the structures they react to. The techniques presented here are either used directly in the following chapters of the work, or are related to them. The basic detectors only consider structures at a specific scale and deliver points without scale information. In section 2.1.2, methods how to obtain scale information given an image location are discussed, and in section 2.1.3, some region detectors are presented.

2.1.1 Point Detectors

Derivative Based Detectors

A common method to detect certain image structures is to use derivative operators or combinations of them. As derivatives are very sensitive against noise, the images typically have to be smoothed using Gaussian filters first. Since convolution and taking the derivative are commutative operations, it is possible to perform the derivation of the Gaussian filter and then to convolve it with the image. This is more efficient, since taking the derivatives has only to be performed for the Gaussian kernel, which is typically much smaller than the entire image.

2 Interest Point Detection

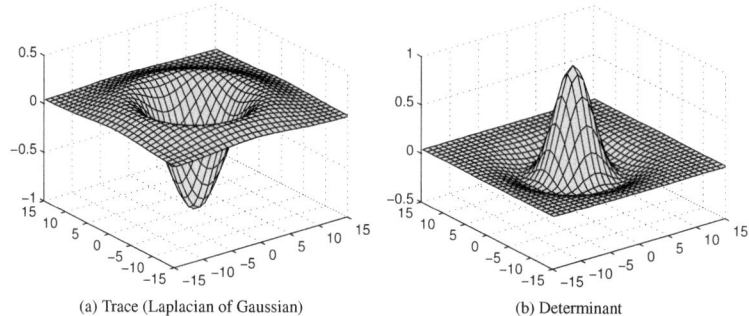

(a) Trace (Laplacian of Gaussian) (b) Determinant

Figure 2.1: Derivative expressions based on the Hessian matrix, applied on a Gaussian function.

The use of Gaussian derivatives as detectors for visually meaningful structures is supported by results from neuro-physiological studies by Young (1987). He states that the visual receptive fields in the primate eye are shaped like a sum of Gaussian derivative like functions.

Differentiation in 2D depends on the direction of the differentiation. If we want to obtain rotation invariant filters, different directional derivatives have to be combined. A complete treatment of differential invariants is out of scope of this work, the reader is instead referred to Lindeberg (1999). There, an overview about invariant combinations of derivatives can be found.

For detecting blob like image structures, a popular choice are differential expressions derived from the Hessian matrix, namely the trace and the determinant. Let $I : \mathbb{R}^2 \rightarrow \mathbb{R}$ be the image intensity function, thus $I(\mathbf{x})$ is the gray value at location $\mathbf{x} = (x, y)^\top$. The Hessian matrix is given by

$$\mathbf{H}(I) = \begin{bmatrix} I_{xx} & I_{xy} \\ I_{yx} & I_{yy} \end{bmatrix}, \quad (2.1)$$

where $I_{xy} = \frac{\partial^2 I}{\partial x \partial y}$. The trace and the determinant of the Hessian matrix are

$$\text{tr}(\mathbf{H}(I)) = I_{xx} + I_{yy} \quad (2.2)$$

and

$$\det(\mathbf{H}(I)) = I_{xx} I_{yy} - I_{xy}^2. \quad (2.3)$$

The trace of the Hessian matrix is the Laplacian. Applying these expressions to a Gaussian function results in the desired image filters for detecting blob like structures. This can be seen intuitively from the graphic representation of these functions in figure 2.1, as both filters have a blob like shape and can act as a matched filter.

Harris and Stephens (1988) proposed a combined corner and edge detector based on the Moravec detector (Moravec, 1977). The basic idea of the Moravec detector is that a small local region around a point will change in a different way whether a flat region, a corner or an edge is present. Intensity values inside a small window centered at the point and a slightly shifted window are compared. The degree of change between the two windows is determined by calculating the *sum of squared differences* (SSD) which is essentially the squared Euclidean norm of the intensity differences of the vectorized image patches,

$$SSD(a,b,\Delta_x,\Delta_y) = \sum_{x=1}^{W}\sum_{y=1}^{H} w_{a,b}(x,y)\left(I(x,y) - I(x-\Delta_x, y-\Delta_y)\right)^2, \quad (2.4)$$

where $w_{a,b}: \mathbb{R}^2 \to [0,1]$ is a windowing function, centered at location (a,b). Δ_x and Δ_y is the shift in the x and y direction. W and H are the image width and height respectively.

Now a set of shifts in several directions is considered. When slightly shifting the window in any direction and a flat region is present, the SSD is small. If an edge is present, the SSD is large, except when the shift direction is consistent with the edge. When a corner is present, the SSD is large for shifts in any direction. The traditional Moravec detector has a number of disadvantages, e.g., the number of shifts considered are limited and the detector lacks rotation invariance, since the window function used is rectangular and binary.

Harris and Stephens overcame some of the limitations by using derivatives for the calculation of the difference in the image signal and they used a circular window function in order to be robust against rotations. The directional derivatives are multiplied and averaged over a local window. The expressions can be summarized in a matrix which looks like

$$\mathbf{M}^{\sigma_I}(I) = G^{\sigma_I} * \begin{bmatrix} I_x^2 & I_x I_y \\ I_y I_x & I_y^2 \end{bmatrix} = \begin{bmatrix} \mu_{11} & \mu_{12} \\ \mu_{21} & \mu_{22} \end{bmatrix}, \quad (2.5)$$

where $I_x = \frac{\partial I}{\partial x}$ and $*$ is the convolution operator. σ_I is the so called "integration scale" and determines the size of the neighborhood considered. The window function is an isotropic, 2D Gaussian function $G^\sigma : \mathbb{R}^2 \to \mathbb{R}$ given by

$$G^\sigma(\mathbf{x}) = G(\mathbf{x};\sigma) = \frac{1}{\sqrt{2\pi\sigma^2}} e^{-\frac{\mathbf{x}^T \mathbf{x}}{2\sigma^2}}. \quad (2.6)$$

The eigenvalues ϵ_1 and ϵ_2 of the matrix M are proportional to the principal curvature of the image surface at that point. The relation of ϵ_1 and ϵ_2 determines whether a corner, an edge or a

2 Interest Point Detection

flat region is present. In order to avoid explicit eigenvalue computation for corner detection, a measure to describe the "cornerness" of a point can be derived as

$$\begin{aligned} \text{cornerness} &= \det(\mathbf{M}) - \kappa \operatorname{tr}(\mathbf{M})^2 \\ &= \epsilon_1 \epsilon_2 - \kappa(\epsilon_1 + \epsilon_2)^2 \\ &= (\mu_{11}\mu_{22} - \mu_{12}^2) - \kappa(\mu_{11} + \mu_{22})^2, \end{aligned} \quad (2.7)$$

where κ is a factor that has to be determined experimentally. By choosing a suitable threshold, corner points can be identified.

Interest point detection based on derivatives or combinations of derivatives is obviously just one possible technique. In the following, we describe another method based on wavelets, with which we have made good experiences.

Wavelet Based Salient Point Detector

Loupias et al. (2000) introduced a wavelet based interest point detector for image retrieval applications. Its output is a *saliency map*, i.e. the pixels in the image are augmented by a saliency value. This measure indicates how strongly the image signal changes over different resolutions. The concept is somewhat different from other interest point detectors in that they typically output a binary decision whether a specific structure is present or not, where the Loupias detector assigns a continuous saliency value to every pixel. Of course, other detectors do also have confidence values for the existence of a particular structure (e.g. corners) at some stage in the detection process. However, finally a decision has to be made whether the desired structure is indeed present. Shifting the decision threshold will either lead to misses of the structure sought, or to wrong detections.

The wavelet based interest point detector is not restricted to finding a special type of structure, yet the patterns found are not random. A design criterion for this detector was that the points with strong response should be distributed over the whole image, and not only be gathered at textured areas and corners. This would be the case if taking, e.g., the gradient magnitude as a saliency measure.

The detector uses a Discrete Wavelet Transform (DWT) as a tool for the multi resolution analysis of a signal. Wavelets are wave like functions with compact support. Given a mother wavelet $\psi : \mathbb{R} \to \mathbb{R}$, a family of wavelet functions can be constructed by dilation s and translation u of this mother wavelet, according to

$$\psi_{s,u}(x) = \frac{1}{\sqrt{s}} \psi\left(\frac{x-u}{s}\right), \quad (2.8)$$

2.1 State-of-the-Art

with

$$\int_{-\infty}^{+\infty} \psi(x)dx = 0. \tag{2.9}$$

The wavelet transformation of the signal $f : \mathbb{R} \to \mathbb{R}$ is

$$(W_s f)(u) = \langle f, \psi_{u,s} \rangle = \frac{1}{\sqrt{s}} \int_{-\infty}^{+\infty} f(x) \psi \left(\frac{x-u}{s} \right) dx. \tag{2.10}$$

The parameters u and s might be continuous, however, this is highly redundant. For the DWT, a set of orthogonal wavelets with a discrete parameterization is used. In particular, dyadic wavelets are considered, where the scaling factor is a power of two:

$$\psi_{j,k}(x) = \frac{1}{\sqrt{2^{-j}}} \psi \left(\frac{x - 2^{-j}k}{2^{-j}} \right), \quad j \in \mathbb{N}, k \in \{0, 1, \ldots, 2^j - 1\}. \tag{2.11}$$

Again, the wavelet coefficients can be obtained by inner products of the signal and the respective wavelet functions.

In order to allow for multi resolution analysis at any scale level, a scaling function $\phi : \mathbb{R} \to \mathbb{R}$ is introduced, which is given by

$$\phi_{j,k}(x) = 2^{j/2} \phi(2^j x - k). \tag{2.12}$$

It is used to represent the information of the original signal which cannot be captured by the wavelet functions up to that particular resolution level. The scaling functions together with the wavelet functions form a basis.

A simple, yet common choice as a basis is the Haar wavelet

$$\psi(x) = \begin{cases} +1 & \text{for } 0 \leq x < \frac{1}{2} \\ -1 & \text{for } \frac{1}{2} \leq x < 1 \\ 0 & \text{otherwise} \end{cases}, \tag{2.13}$$

together with a unit scaling function

$$\phi(x) = \begin{cases} 1 & \text{for } 0 \leq x < 1 \\ 0 & \text{otherwise} \end{cases}. \tag{2.14}$$

The functions can be seen from figure 2.2. The wavelet and the scaling functions can be regarded as high-pass and low-pass filters. In practice, the wavelet transform is implemented as a recursive

2 Interest Point Detection

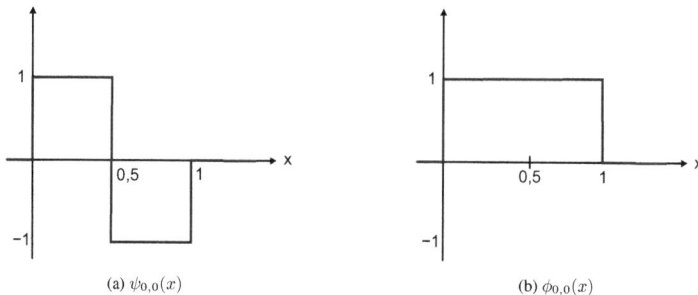

(a) $\psi_{0,0}(x)$ (b) $\phi_{0,0}(x)$

Figure 2.2: Haar wavelet and scaling function.

filtering operation. The signal is subject to a high pass (wavelet) and to a low pass (scaling) filter and the results sampled down. The operation is applied recursively to the low pass filtered signal.

The extension to the 2D case is straightforward, the two dimensional wavelet and scaling functions can be generated from outer products of the one dimensional functions:

$$\begin{aligned}
\phi(x,y) &= \phi(x)\phi(y), \\
\psi^{HL}(x,y) &= \phi(x)\psi(y), \\
\psi^{LH}(x,y) &= \psi(x)\phi(y), \\
\psi^{HH}(x,y) &= \psi(x)\psi(y).
\end{aligned} \quad (2.15)$$

For a two dimensional wavelet transform, the data can be arranged as shown in figure 2.3. The filtering process is repeated iteratively for the down sampled image signal in sub-band LL. Each iteration is referred to as decomposition stage. An example for a final decomposition can be seen in figure 2.4. More details about general wavelet theory can be found, e.g., in Mallat (1989) or Daubechies (1992).

The following description of the wavelet based salient point detector follows Loupias et al. (2000). A signal f is studied at a number of scales $2^{-j}, j \in \mathbb{N}$, and thus is subject to a wavelet transform. High values of j correspond to a coarse, low values to a fine resolution. The wavelet coefficients $W_{2^{-j}}f$ are obtained as described above.

The points we are interested in are those where the signal changes over multiple resolutions. A change in signal is indicated by a high wavelet coefficient. A wavelet coefficient $(W_{2^{-j}}f)(k)$ at a coarse resolution with high absolute value corresponds to a region with high global variation. Since wavelets with compact support are used, one can determine the wavelet coefficients at scale 2^{-j} which correspond to a wavelet coefficient at a coarser scale 2^{-j+1}. These coefficients are called the children of the coefficient $(W_{2^{-j}}f)(k)$.

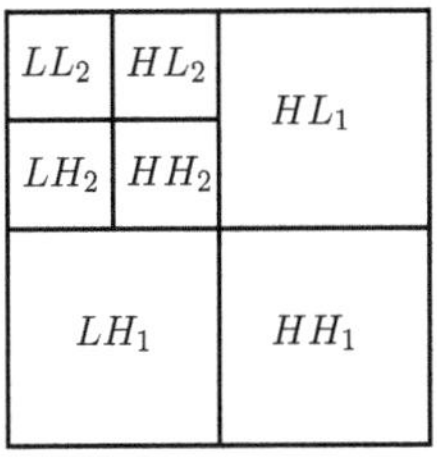

LL_2	HL_2	HL_1
LH_2	HH_2	
LH_1		HH_1

Figure 2.3: A possible arrangement of wavelet coefficients at the second decomposition stage.

In order to obtain the most salient points in the original function, in the set of children of a wavelet coefficient, the one with the highest absolute value gets traced to a finer resolution. This process is repeated until scale 2^{-1} is reached. A coefficient at this level is again based on a number of samples in the original function, depending on the wavelet function used. From these points, the one with the highest gradient in the original function is chosen. The sum of all wavelet coefficients traced until an original image point is reached is referred to as its *saliency value*.

As we deal with 2D images, we trace horizontal (HL), vertical (LH) and diagonal (HH) subbands individually. Tracing is only performed within one direction. In figure 2.4, the tracing of a coefficient is shown for the HL sub-bands. Whenever a final image point is chosen multiple times as the result of tracing individual coefficients or filter directions, the highest value is assigned to that point.

The original detector does not achieve rotation invariance. However, a good robustness against rotation can be obtained by taking the maximum of the directional saliency values.

By tracing all wavelet coefficients, a saliency map of the entire image can be produced. An example saliency map can be seen on the bottom in figure 2.5. The brightness of the pixels is related to their saliency values. The saliency map can be thresholded to obtain points where the signal changes sufficiently over several scales or the N most salient points might be selected. In this work, Haar wavelets as defined in equation (2.13) are used as wavelet functions. Although a multi resolution representation of the image is used in the analysis phase, no scale information is provided by the original detector.

2.1.2 Scale Selection Methods

In order to calculate features, it is necessary to determine the area around an interest point which should be used for computation. In a general object class recognition task, we usually have

2 Interest Point Detection

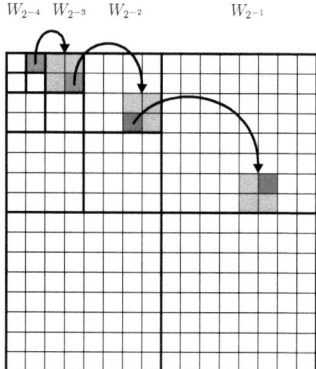

Figure 2.4: Tracing of wavelet coefficients.

no prior knowledge about the scale of the objects. Interest points with scale information are highly beneficial in order to be invariant or at least robust towards scale changes of the object. Otherwise we would have to extract features at many different scales, which would increase the number of features and introduce additional ambiguities.

We first review general methods for scale selection and then describe some example detectors.

Scale-space Representation

As formulated by Lindeberg (1999), a general idea for scale selection is to build a linear *scale space*. A linear scale space representation $L : \mathbb{R}^N \times \mathbb{R}_+ \to \mathbb{R}$ for an N-dimensional signal $f : \mathbb{R}^N \to \mathbb{R}$ is formally defined as the solution of the diffusion equation

$$L_t = \frac{1}{2} \sum_{i=1}^{N} L_{x_i x_i}, \qquad (2.16)$$

with initial condition $L(\mathbf{x}; 0) = f(\mathbf{x})$. Again, $L_t = \frac{\partial L}{\partial t}$ and $L_{x_i x_i} = \frac{\partial^2 L}{\partial x_i \partial x_i}$. The parameter t, which refers to "time" in the original diffusion equation can be interpreted as scale in the context of images.

Alternatively, a linear scale space can be constructed by convolving the image signal with Gaussian kernels G of various width, i.e.

$$L(\mathbf{x}; t) = G(\mathbf{x}; \sqrt{t}) * f(\mathbf{x}), \qquad (2.17)$$

2.1 State-of-the-Art

Figure 2.5: Wavelet based salient points: sample image and corresponding saliency map. Brighter pixels correspond to more salient points.

2 Interest Point Detection

where the N-dimensional Gaussian kernel $G : \mathbb{R}^N \times \mathbb{R}_+ \setminus \{0\} \to \mathbb{R}$ is defined as

$$G(\mathbf{x}, \sigma) = \frac{1}{(2\pi\sigma^2)^{N/2}} e^{-\frac{\mathbf{x}^\top \mathbf{x}}{2\sigma^2}} \tag{2.18}$$

Please note that in Lindebergs formulation, the measure of the scale is in units of variance, i.e. $t = \sigma^2$, and thus the parameter for the width of the Gaussian kernel in equation (2.17) must be $\sigma = \sqrt{t}$.

In the case of a two dimensional image function I, we obtain a three dimensional scale space. As shown in the previous section, differential expressions can be used in order to detect interesting structures in a signal. These structures can now be detected together with the scale information by calculating scale normalized spatial derivatives on the different scale space layers and then searching for maxima in the entire volume. The normalization has to be performed, because the amplitude of spatial derivatives generally decreases over time. For this purpose, Lindeberg introduces a scale normalized derivative operator, where the normalization factor depends on the order of the differentiation in the respective spatial direction. Details on the normalization process can be found in Lindeberg (1994).

Typically, not the whole scale space is searched for maxima, since the computation of the derivatives at all possible scale space layers might be very time consuming. Instead, candidate locations are found on some scale space planes and maxima are searched over the scale dimension at this particular location. If necessary, the spatial locations have to be refined.

A variety of scale invariant detectors rely on a scale space representation as described above. Especially to mention is Mikolajczyk and Schmid (2002) with the Hessian-Laplace and the Harris-Laplace detector, as well as Lowe (2004) with the Difference of Gaussian (DoG) detector used in the well known SIFT (Scale Invariant Feature Transform) framework. The DoG kernel approximates the LoG kernel and allows a fast implementation. However, also other techniques for scale selection exist. They are described briefly in the next section in order to give an idea about them.

Other Techniques

Alternative approaches to scale selection have been described lately by Jurie and Schmid (2004), Tuytelaars and Van Gool (2004), Matas et al. (2002) or Dorko and Schmid (2006).

In the *Maximally Stable Extremal Regions* (MSER) approach by Matas et al. (2002), images are converted to binary representations using a number of different thresholds. In these binary images, connected components are searched for, and the areas that are stable over a large number of thresholds are selected. This approach delivers arbitrary shaped regions that are covariant under affine transformations. Ellipses can be fitted to these regions in order to reduce storage cost and to simplify further processing.

Tuytelaars and Van Gool (2000) presented a method called *Intensity-Based Regions* (IBR) for wide baseline stereo matching. In this method, intensity extrema are searched in an image via a non maximum suppression algorithm. From these seed points on, the vicinity of the points gets scanned along rays. Maxima of an evaluation function along the rays are linked together and determine the area borders of the region. Typically, ellipses are fitted around the areas.

Dorko and Schmid (2006) have presented a scale selection mechanism based on a region descriptor. They test if the features extracted from consecutive scales are stable. They use the SIFT descriptor and Laplacian as well as multi scale Harris interest points, calculated at several predefined scales. They look for scales where the descriptors remain similar for consecutive scales, i.e. they search for *maximally stable local descriptions*. The motivation for their approach to scale selection was that the descriptors might change noticeably even when the scale changes only little. When now the descriptor itself is used for scale selection, the process might benefit from properties of the descriptor, e.g. illumination invariance and robustness to noise. A disadvantage of this approach is that scale selection is tied to the descriptor used later on.

2.1.3 Region Detectors

The detectors used in the course of this work are scale invariant versions of the Harris corner detector and the Hessian detector, as well as the Difference of Gaussian detector. They do not only detect points, but also the scale of the structure under consideration. An interest point changes to a region of interest. By knowing the scale of a structure, the calculation of scale invariant features becomes possible. Despite possessing interesting properties, the original wavelet based detector by Loupias et al. did not provide scale information, which restricted its use four our purposes. For this reason, we extend this detector to provide scale information in section 2.2.

Harris-Laplace and Hessian-Laplace

The Harris and the Hessian detector were extended to be scale invariant by Mikolajczyk and Schmid (2004) and termed Harris-Laplace and Hessian-Laplace respectively. The original equations for the detectors (see equations (2.1) and (2.5)) were extended so that the derivatives are calculated by Gaussian derivative kernels in a scale invariant way.

The scale invariant Harris detector now looks like

$$\mathbf{M}^{\sigma_I,\sigma_D}(I) = \sigma_D^2 G^{\sigma_I} * \begin{bmatrix} (I_x^{\sigma_D})^2 & I_x^{\sigma_D} I_y^{\sigma_D} \\ I_y^{\sigma_D} I_x^{\sigma_D} & (I_y^{\sigma_D})^2 \end{bmatrix}, \tag{2.19}$$

where σ_D is the differentiation scale, i.e. in this context $I_x^{\sigma_D}$ means that the derivative in the direction x is calculated via a Gaussian derivative kernel with scale σ_D. σ_I is the integration scale used for summing the contributions in a scale adapted window.

2 Interest Point Detection

This scale invariant detector is used to find candidate points at several, crude scale space layers. The precise scale is then determined by multiplying LoG functions with the scale space layer at different scales in the range between the previously computed layers. The maximum value of the evaluation is used to compute a new cornerness measure in the vicinity of the respective point, at this scale. The spatial location of the maximum of the cornerness measure is compared to the previous position of the point under consideration. If the spatial location changed, the process is repeated with the new position of that point, until no changes occur.

The scale invariant Hessian detector is given by

$$\mathbf{H}^{\sigma_D}(I) = \begin{bmatrix} I^{\sigma_D}_{xx} & I^{\sigma_D}_{xy} \\ I^{\sigma_D}_{yx} & I^{\sigma_D}_{yy} \end{bmatrix}, \tag{2.20}$$

and the detection process works analogous to the Harris-Laplace detector. Again, $I^{\sigma_D}_{xy}$ means that the second derivatives in the x and y direction were computed using a Gaussian derivative operator at scale σ_D.

For finding maxima, the determinant of the matrix gets evaluated and has to be normalized by σ_D^2 as explained in section 2.1.2. Mikolajczyk et al. (2005b) also describe an affine adaption process. In our basic experiments, we do not consider affine invariance, since it has been shown (for example in Haasdonk (2005)), that the discriminative power of features can decrease when a too large degree of invariance is applied. We restricted ourselves to the use of planar views of the objects, so scale invariance is sufficient. For extended experiments concerning the retrieval of objects in any pose (see Skibbe, 2008, in chapter 10) affine invariant interest points were used.

Difference of Gaussian Detector

The Difference of Gaussian (DoG) detector was proposed by Lowe (1999). The LoG scale space is approximated by DoGs to be implemented more efficiently. For that, an image gets smoothed repeatedly by Gaussian filters, which is the same as convolving the image with Gaussian filters at larger scales. Successive image layers get subtracted from each other, and maxima are searched for in the DoG scale space in a 26 neighborhood. Whenever the effective Gaussian smoothing factor σ is doubled (this is called an *octave*), both the image and the Gaussian kernel are subsampled by the factor of 2, to further speed up computations.

In the original algorithm, a variety of subsequent steps are performed, e.g., the removal of badly localized points on edges. Lowe also assigns an orientation to the points as the dominant gradient direction of the area around the point. This orientation is needed to be able to attach a coordinate system to the point in order to calculate the SIFT features. These features are localized histograms of Gaussian weighted gradient directions, they are explained in detail in section 3.3.3.

2.2 Extension of the Wavelet Based Interest Point Detector

The wavelet based interest point detector described in section 2.1.1 has some advantages compared to other interest point detectors: the number of points retrieved can be controlled easily by taking the N most salient points, and these N points are usually spread out over the whole image and do not cluster in few regions. For some object class recognition strategies, it is important to have a sufficient number of interest points (see Nowak et al., 2006), and they should cover all interesting structures in an image. The original Loupias detector does not provide scale information, which make it inferior compared to other detectors. We thus extend the Loupias detector to provide this information.

Although the DWT delivers a multi scale representation of the image, it is not equivalent to the linear scale space representation as described in section 2.1.2, since in the DWT, we are restricted to orthogonal wavelets with compact support. The Gaussian kernel as needed for a linear scale space does not fulfill this condition. To still obtain scale information, we propose to apply a Laplacian scale selection to the points delivered by the original detector. We thus name the detector *Loupias-Laplace* detector.

In order to infer the scale of local structures, we use the scale normalized Laplacian kernel at the points initially found by the original Loupias detector,

$$\text{Lap}^t = t(L_{xx}^t + L_{yy}^t). \tag{2.21}$$

By L^t, a specific scale space layer is referred to, i.e. $L_{xx}^t(\mathbf{x}) = L_{xx}(\mathbf{x};t)$, $\mathbf{x} = (x,y)^\top$. The expression has to be normalized, since otherwise the maxima would decrease with increasing scale. As the scale space representation is constructed by convolution with Gaussian filters at increasing scales, we use Laplacian of Gaussian (LoG) filters at different scales and apply it to the points in the image. As the unit of the scale space is in variances, the LoG kernel has to be normalized by the variance of the Gaussian, i.e. σ^2. The LoG kernel is visualized in figure 2.1, it is the same as the trace of the Hessian matrix.

From these filter responses, the maximum is searched and the respective scale used as scale for the local structure. As a stability criterion for the maximum search, it can be required that the maximum must be above a certain threshold. It is also possible to allow multiple maxima, when they are isolated within a certain scale range. Then the point is added multiple times to the set of interest points, with multiple scales.

For blobs, the maximum of the scale space function is reached when σ is proportional to the blob size. For step edges, the extremum of the Laplacian scale selection function is reached with σ equal to the distance to the step edge. An analytical proof for this can be found in Lindeberg (1994). The scale of a point on an edge is determined by its vicinity. It gives information about the scale of a structure in relation to its surrounding.

2 Interest Point Detection

The algorithm is described in algorithm 2.1. The output of the detector is set of local areas $\mathbf{o} = (x, y, s)^\top$, where x, y are the coordinates and s is the scale of an interest point.

Algorithm 2.1: Loupias-Laplace interest point detector

Input: Intensity image I; number of desired regions N'; optional: default scale σ_d;
Output: $\mathbf{S} = \{\mathbf{o}_1, \ldots, \mathbf{o}_N\}$; $N \leq N'$ $\mathbf{o} = (x, y, s)^\top$;
Initialization: Create a filter bank $\mathbf{B}$ of normalized LoG filters: $\mathbf{B} = \{\text{LoG}^{\sigma_1}, \ldots, \text{LoG}^{\sigma_M}\}$;
begin
  // Calculate the saliency map of image I:
  $\mathbf{M} \longleftarrow \texttt{calculateSaliencyMap}\,(I)$;
  // Obtain a list of points in decreasing order of the saliency
  // values, i.e. $\mathbf{S}' = \{\mathbf{o}'_1, \ldots, \mathbf{o}'_K | \text{sal}(\mathbf{o}'_\ell) \geq \text{sal}(\mathbf{o}'_{\ell+1})\}$, $\mathbf{o}' = (x, y)^\top$:
  $\mathbf{S}' \longleftarrow \texttt{getIptsSortedBySaliencyValue}\,(\mathbf{M})$;
  foreach $\mathbf{o}'_i \in \mathbf{S}'$ **do**
    // Evaluate the LoG filter responses at point $\mathbf{o}'_i$, store the results in a vector $\mathbf{v}_i$:
    for $k \longleftarrow 1$ **to** M **do**
      $v_{i,k} \longleftarrow \texttt{getFilterResponse}\,(I(\mathbf{o}'_i), \text{LoG}^{\sigma_k})$;
    end
    // Search for the maximum in $\mathbf{v}_i$, store the respective index in h_i:
    $h_i \longleftarrow \texttt{getIndexOfMaximum}\,(\mathbf{v}_i)$;
    if $\texttt{validMaximumFound}\,(\mathbf{v}_i, h_i)$ **then**
      // Add the point with the respective scale σ_{h_i} to the output list:
      $\mathbf{S} \longleftarrow \mathbf{S} \cup \{(\mathbf{o}_i, \sigma_{h_i})\}$;
      // stop the evaluation if the desired number of regions is found
      if $|\mathbf{S}| = N'$ **then break**;
    else
      // When desired: assign a default scale σ_d, otherwise discard the point
      if $\texttt{paramGiven}\,(\sigma_d)$ **then**
        $\mathbf{S} \longleftarrow \mathbf{S} \cup \{(\mathbf{o}_i, \sigma_d)\}$;
        // stop the evaluation if the desired number of regions is found
        if $|\mathbf{S}| = N'$ **then break**;
      end
    end
  end
end

With this procedure, no scale invariance in a strict mathematical sense is obtained, since the initial interest point positions might differ slightly depending on the pose of the object. However, significant robustness towards scale changes can be obtained, as will be shown in the next section.

2.3 Experimental Evaluation

In this section, we want to compare the properties and the performance of some commonly used detectors, especially in relation to our newly proposed Loupias-Laplace detector. For every interest point detector, the ability to find reoccurring structures is a prerequisite. Yet strict repeatability is not the only criterion if we focus on object class recognition. It is also important to retrieve *characteristic* object parts, even if they are not always at the same (relative) position. For example, points on an edge have a weak repeatability, since they are not localized well along the edge. However, they still can carry important information about the object. In this respect, the results for detector repeatability and accuracy are only given for completeness reasons, they are not the most important tests in an object retrieval setting. More meaningful are the test regarding the number and kind of structures obtained by the detectors from the images, as well as the suitability of the detections for an object class recognition task.

2.3.1 Repeatability and Accuracy

The first evaluation is done in terms of *repeatability* and *accuracy* of the localization. The test follows a protocol proposed by Mikolajczyk et al. (2005b). There, a standard test set of images consisting of scenes subject to scale and viewpoint change, blur, jpeg artifacts and illumination change is introduced. Since the detectors that we want to test are not affine invariant, we skipped the images concerning viewpoint change. For each distortion type, there are six images available in different degradation stages. Precise homographies between these images are known, so that point correspondences can be evaluated. The different kinds of distortions have been applied both to textured as well as to structured scenes. Samples of the test images are displayed in figure 2.6.

The repeatability of a detector is measured by the number of common regions in two images, the accuracy of a match is measured by the overlap error. Both aspects are combined in the evaluation, since the repeatability of covariant areas with an overlap error below a certain threshold is measured. The overlap is computed by projecting the detected area $\mathbf{K}_M$ from the test image onto the reference image using the known homography $\mathbf{H}$ between the images. $\mathbf{M}$ is a 2×2 matrix describing a circular region, $\mathbf{M} = \frac{1}{s^2}\mathbf{1}_2$, with s being the scale (=radius) of the region. The region $\mathbf{K}_M$ is given as $\mathbf{K}_M = \{\mathbf{x} \in \mathbb{R}^2 | \mathbf{x}^\top \mathbf{M} \mathbf{x} \leq 1\}$. Then the overlap error between region $\mathbf{K}_{M_a}$ and $\mathbf{K}_{M_b}$ is defined as

$$\mathrm{OE}(\mathbf{K}_{M_b}, \mathbf{K}_{M_a}) = 1 - \frac{\mathbf{K}_{M_a} \cap \mathbf{K}_{(\mathbf{H}^\top \mathbf{M}_b \mathbf{H})}}{\mathbf{K}_{M_a} \cup \mathbf{K}_{(\mathbf{H}^\top \mathbf{M}_b \mathbf{H})}}. \quad (2.22)$$

Only those areas that can be projected onto the other image plane are taken into account. These sets shall be denoted as $\mathbf{R}_1$ and $\mathbf{R}_2$ for the respective images. The function $c(\mathbf{R}_1, \mathbf{R}_2, \varepsilon)$ measures the number of corresponding regions with an overlap error smaller than ε, $|\mathbf{R}|$ is the cardinality of the set $\mathbf{R}$.

2 Interest Point Detection

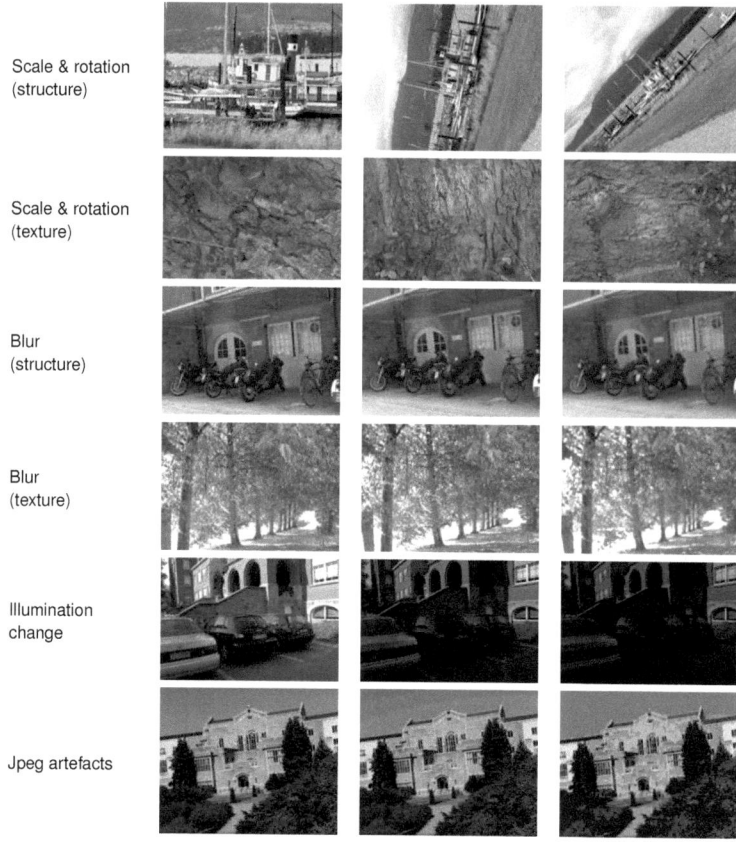

Figure 2.6: Sample test images in different degradation stages (source: Mikolajczyk et al., 2005b).

2.3 Experimental Evaluation

Then the repeatability score RS is defined as

$$\text{RS}(\mathbf{R}_1, \mathbf{R}_2, \varepsilon) = \frac{c(\mathbf{R}_1, \mathbf{R}_2, \varepsilon)}{\min(|\mathbf{R}_1|, |\mathbf{R}_2|)}, \qquad (2.23)$$

for an overlap error smaller than ε. In the standard evaluation protocol as in our tests, ε is fixed to 40%. When calculating the overlap error, the reference area has to be scaled to a standard size, in order to not be biased against the overall size of the detected areas. Detectors delivering bigger areas would have an advantage, since for larger scales, the overlap error decreases. For evaluation, we use the matlab evaluation code provided by Mikolajczyk et al. (2005b)[1] in order to be comparable to previously published results. Further details about the evaluation process can be found there. In the original work, solely affine invariant detectors were tested.

In a first test we want to verify that the scale selection procedure for our Loupias-Laplace detector is indeed effective, so we compare the results for the standard Loupias detector with a fixed radius of 15 pixels to the Loupias-Laplace detector with scale information. Since the allowed overlap error is fixed to be below 40%, beginning from a scale factor of $\frac{1}{\sqrt{0.6}} \approx 1.291$, no regions can be matched any more for the fixed radii, the repeatability score has to be zero then. Everything matched beyond this scale is due to the scale selection process. In figure 2.7, we have summarized the results for the scenes concerning scale change (bark and boat). For very moderate scale changes, where the overlap error for regions with a fixed radius is still below the required threshold, the repeatability rate for fixed scale points is higher than for points with Laplacian scale selection. For the fixed radii, of course no scale errors occur when the threshold is low enough. The results beyond this threshold show that the scale selection process is indeed successful. Figure 2.7 demonstrates that the Laplacian scale selection enables matching of areas even for quite large scale changes (up to a factor of 4 in our tests).

In the following experiments, we test the repeatability of our extended detector in comparison to the DoG detector, the Hessian-Laplace as well as the Harris-Laplace detector and the Kadir & Bradey Salient Region detector. The choice was motivated by the fact that these detectors are commonly used in image retrieval and detection algorithms and reference implementations by the authors exist.

The different detectors (besides the Loupias-Laplace detector) deliver a different number of regions, depending on the particular scene type. This is intuitively clear, since the detectors respond to different structures that may be present in the images to varying degrees. The repeatability rate is implicitly sensitive to the number of detected areas. When too many regions are detected, they might be matched accidentally because of their density. When the threshold for certain detectors is set very firm, only few, but very stable regions might be detected, boosting the repeatability rate in an unfair way. Thus we used the standard parameter settings for the detectors and set the number of regions for the Loupias Laplace detector to a similar range as the

---

[1] http://www.robots.ox.ac.uk/~vgg/research/affine

2 Interest Point Detection

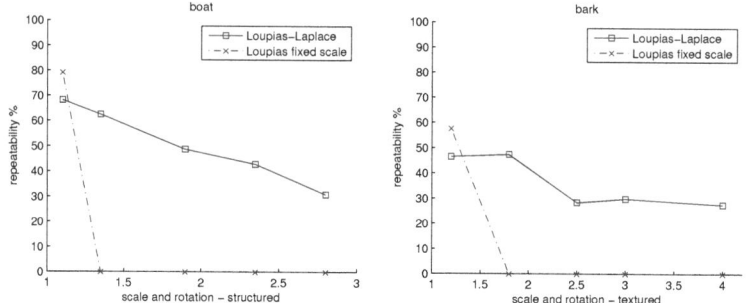

Figure 2.7: Repeatability scores for the Loupias Laplace detector and the Loupias detector with fixed radius.

other detectors. In particular, we took the average number of detections for the Hessian-Laplace and Harris-Laplace detector, since they are most similar from a conceptual point of view.

Figure 2.8 shows the results for the different detectors and scene types, at different degradations stages. The Hessian-Laplace detector together with the DoG detector proves to deliver comparatively stable regions. The DoG detector seems to be sensitive against blur in textured scenes. The Loupias-Laplace detector performs well for blur, illumination change and jpeg compression, however is less stable against rotation and scale change. As mentioned in section 2.1.1, the basic detector is not rotation invariant, but only possesses a robustness against rotation. The repeatability score for the Kadir & Bradey detector is generally lower than the others, however, it has been shown that this detector is very efficient in an object class detection setting as evaluated in Mikolajczyk and Schmid (2005). The test shows that the repeatability score for the Loupias-Laplace detector is in a similar range than the other detectors tested. The detector is thus suitable for object recognition tasks. The test was included to verify that the basic requirement for an interest point operator, i.e. to repeatedly find similar points under various conditions, is met. Yet the repeatability is not the only criterion if we focus on object class recognition. In the following, we thus also test other characteristics, like the variety of structures to be found or the performance in an object retrieval setting.

2.3.2 Structure Variety

The next test performed is concerned with the variety of structures extracted from the detected regions. In order to be able to deal with the mass of features extracted, they are typically clustered in an intermediate processing step, see chapter 4. For this reason, we test the clustering properties of features extracted from the local areas identified by the different detectors.

2.3 Experimental Evaluation

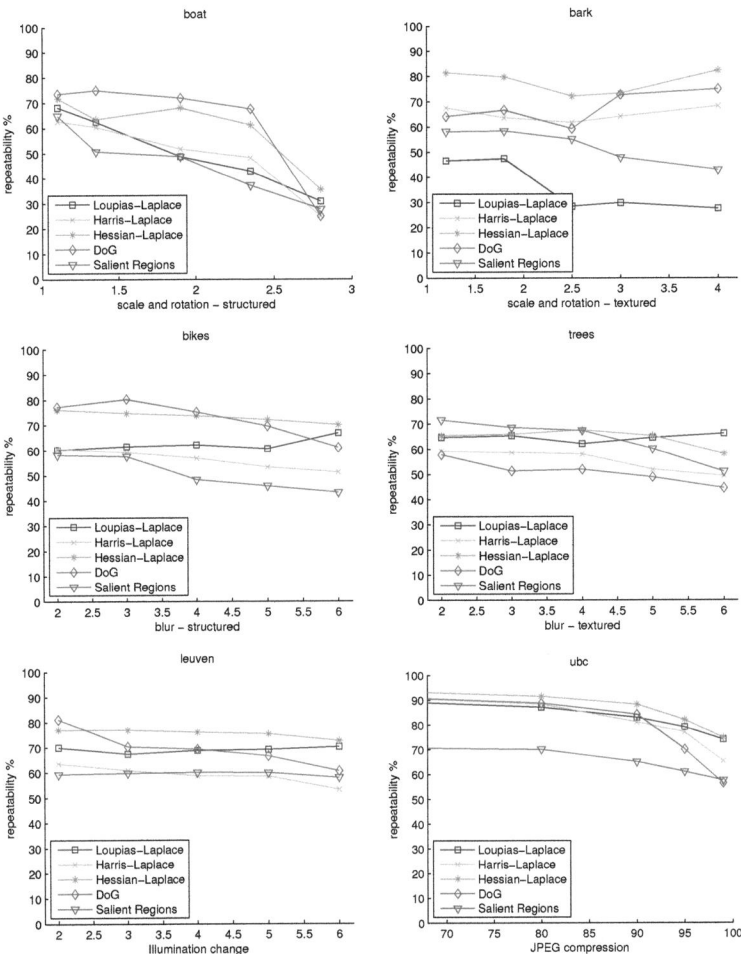

Figure 2.8: Repeatability scores for different detectors and imaging conditions.

2 Interest Point Detection

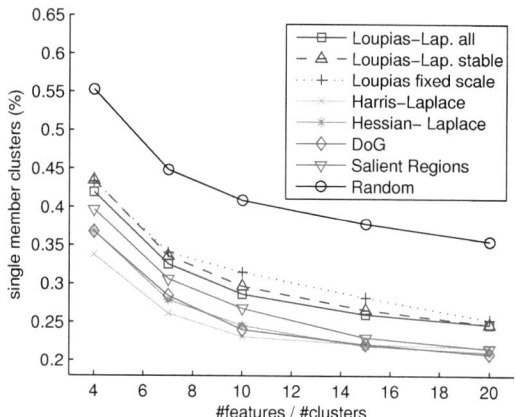

Figure 2.9: Single member clusters.

The database used for the following tests is a challenging set of 1300 animal pictures belonging to 14 animal classes. The animals in the pictures are photographed in diverse poses, sizes and in front of different backgrounds. This dataset was proposed by the MUSCLE initiative (Hanbury and Targhi, 2006), and is a subset of the Corel database. Full segmentation masks for the animals are available, however, since our method does not require segmentation, we do not use it. The animal types present are: cheetah (34), cougar (100), coyote (100), deer (86), dog (200), elephant (100), goat (100), hippopotamus (41), horse (200), leopard (66), lion (100), moose (14), rhinoceros (59) and tiger (100). The images are all of size 256×384. We choose three different types of features capturing different properties of an area. The features were concatenated and normalized so that each feature range was between 0 and 1. For color, we used an HSV color histogram with quantization factors $8 \times 4 \times 3$ for the respective layers. The local shape of the patch was captured by a SIFT-like gradient location and direction histogram (Lowe, 2004), here we used a 3×3 grid for the location and 6 orientations. To capture texture information, we calculated the mean of the wavelet coefficients corresponding to a detected region at the three largest scales and the three orientations. A large value of such a feature means a rough texture, a small value describes a smooth region. All features were concatenated, so the altogether feature dimension for each local area was 159. More details on the features can be found in chapter 3.

The test closely follows one proposed in Mikolajczyk et al. (2005a). In order to be comparable to the results reported there, we use agglomerative clustering (see chapter 4) with average linkage. We extracted features from 30,000 randomly selected regions detected by a respective detector. In the process of clustering, a tree is build by joining the clusters with the shortest distance.

Following the experiments in Mikolajczyk et al. (2005a), the trees were cut at several levels, given by specific ratios of detections versus the number of clusters (i.e. 4, 7, 10, 15, 20).

In addition to the detectors tested in the previous section, we also examine features obtained from random regions (random locations at random scales) in the image, in order to verify that it is beneficial to use interest point detectors at all. We also included features calculated from the original Loupias detector with a fixed radius of 15 pixels. This is referred to as *Loupias fixed scale* in the experiments. We tested two variants of the Loupias-Laplace detector. In the first method, whenever no distinct scale could be determined for a point, it is discarded. This detector is termed *Loupias-Laplace stable*. The other option is to use a default radius. This method is referred to as *Loupias-Laplace all*. For all detectors, regions smaller than 5 pixels radius were discarded, since we deem them too unstable for calculating texture and shape information.

The test measures the percentage of clusters with just one member. Since we use agglomerative clustering where always the closest clusters are merged, the single member clusters are distinct and noticeably different from features belonging to bigger clusters. The single cluster ratios for the different detectors and cut values are listed in figure 2.9.

We can see that the features extracted from the Loupias-Laplace regions are more diverse than features from the Harris-Laplace, the Hessian-Laplace or the DoG regions, since more single member clusters exist. The Loupias-Laplace detectors does not only extract a specific image structure (e.g. blobs), but a larger variety. As expected, the Loupias detector without scale selection shows a higher single cluster ratio than the detectors with scale selection. Since the scale information of the local structures is not considered, the regions obtained are more diverse. Regions extracted from random areas are very distinct, as indicated by the high single cluster ratio. For these structures, it is difficult to find a compact representation.

The diverse types of structures retrieved by the different detectors can be seen from example images in figure 2.10. There, the regions detected by the individual detectors are shown. For the Harris-Laplace, the Hessian-Laplace, the Kadir & Bradey Salient Region detector and the DoG detector, the same settings were used as for the repeatability experiments. Where the number of areas to be detected could be specified, they were set to 500. The images are displayed in gray scale, since all detectors only rely on gray scale information.

For the Harris-Laplace and the Hessian-Laplace detectors, the number of detections varies tremendously for the different types of images. Smooth image parts (e.g., the unsharp background of the cheetah image) are covered only very sparsely. For certain classification approaches, in particular bag-of-feature type methods, a sufficient number of detected regions is vital. This aspect is examined in further detail in the next section. The DoG detector delivers a very large number of regions, however, they are very small. Of course, the size of the detection and the area where features are computed do not have to be the same. We have to distinguish two kinds of scales: the scale of the interest point detection, e.g., the width of the gradient filter, and the scale of the feature extraction. They might be related by a factor different from one. In this visualization, the sizes are displayed as given by the detectors, in order to compare them better.

2 Interest Point Detection

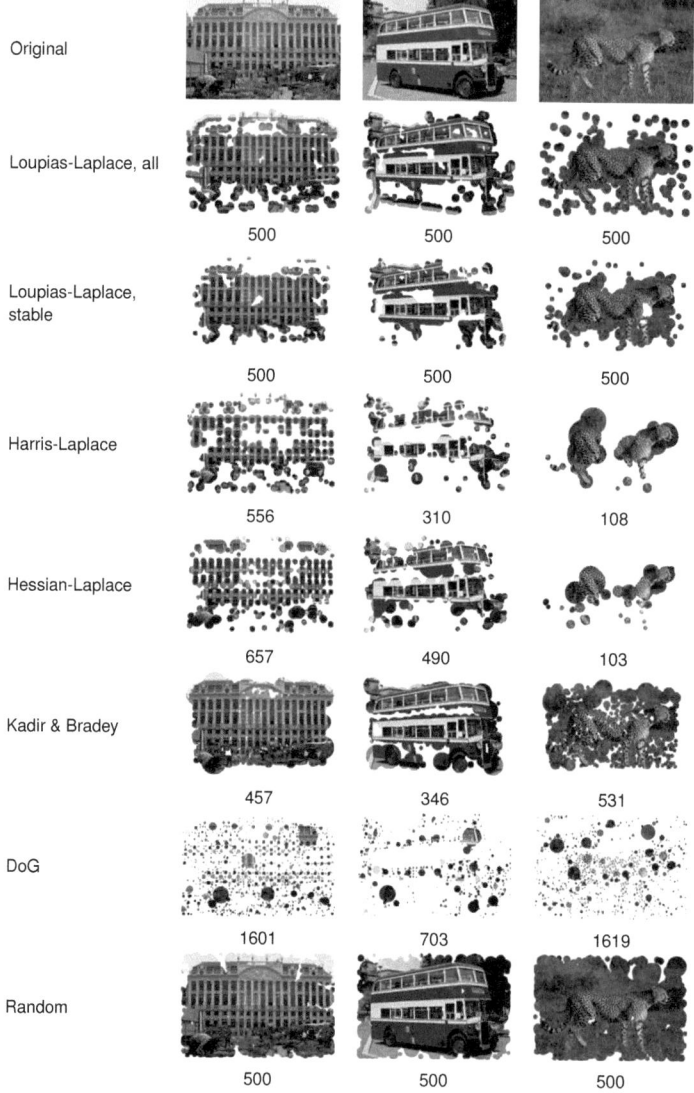

Figure 2.10: Types of areas detected by different detectors. Below the images, the number of detections are shown. The original images are from the 60k Corel db (Li and Wang, 2003).

The Loupias-Laplace regions cover all important structures in the image, especially when using a default scale for the regions where the scale selection process was not successful.

2.3.3 Object Classification

Our actual goal is to use the detectors in object classification tasks. So we want to compare the performance of the detectors in this respect. As database, we use the animal collection introduced in the previous section. We choose a bag-of-features (Csurka et al., 2004) classification approach, where histograms of cluster memberships of the individual local features are compared. The histogram creation process is described formally in section 7. The codebooks are again obtained via agglomerative clustering, with the cut value set to 4,000 cluster centers in order to have similar histogram sizes. Clusters consisting of a single member were discarded. The histograms are classified with a standard multi class Support Vector Machine (SVM) (Schölkopf and Smola, 2001) in a one-vs-one mode. We used the libSVMTL[2] implementation. A histogram intersection kernel was used. The results were obtained using five-fold cross validation and the results averaged over the runs.

A beneficial property of the Loupias-Laplace detector is that the number of points retrieved can be controlled easily by considering the N most salient points. The quality of the histograms obtained from the local features do not only depend on the type of the detected structures, but also on the number of them. Few detections result in very sparse histograms that might be unstable for classification. As shown in section 2.3.2, some of the standard detectors deliver very few regions, because they only focus on a certain type of structure. Changing thresholds changes to what extent structures are considered to be of the desired type, however, only in a certain range. We evaluated the classification performance for the different detectors in relation to the average number of regions detected in the images. For the Harris-Laplace, the Hessian-Laplace and the Kadir & Bradey Salient Region detector, we used the standard parameter setting as used for repeatability experiments, as well as the lowest threshold we could tune, resulting in an increased number of detections. The DoG detector did not offer this opportunity, so only a single result is listed. We increased the scale of the DoG detections by a factor of two, since initially they are very small, and only few detections could pass the required minimum radius of 5 pixels. For the other detectors, the number of regions considered per image was adjusted to 200, 500, 1,000, 1,500 and 2,000. As a baseline, we also computed the color, shape and texture features from the entire image and used these global features directly for classification.

Classification results depending on the average number of detected regions per image can be seen from figure 2.11. The best results could be obtained from the Loupias-Laplace all detector. Generally speaking, an increased number of detections results in more stable histograms and thus better classification rates. The DoG detector mainly delivered very small regions. Even after scaling them by a factor of 2, only few regions could pass the the required minimum radius of 5 pixels to be considered. The Harris-Laplace detector also delivers comparatively few regions,

---

[2]http://lmb.informatik.uni-freiburg.de/lmbsoft/libsvmtl/

2 Interest Point Detection

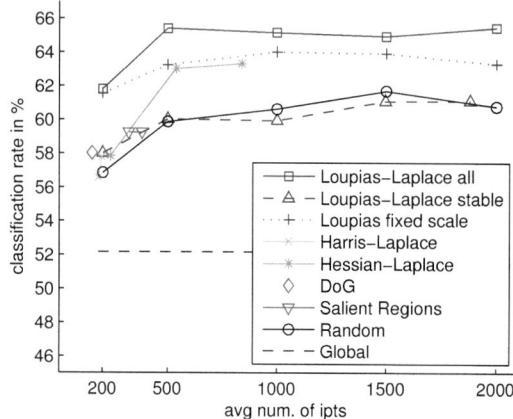

Figure 2.11: Classification results for the different detectors, depending on the number of interest points obtained.

still after lowering the detection threshold. An interesting observation is that a large number of random regions could even outperform some of the sophisticated detectors. This observation is consistent with the results of Nowak et al. (2006). There, they report superior classification results for a sufficient number of random detections compared to the LoG and the Harris-Laplace detector. The setting is similar to ours, as they also use a bag-of-features paradigm.

All part based approaches are superior to the baseline result using global descriptors. This shows the overall capability of using local representations. In particular, calculating texture and structure information from the entire image is not discriminative enough, since the entire image is not uniform, and observations from different regions get intermixed.

Incorporating context information in the form of background detections improves the classification rate. The reason is that the background and the animal class are of course somewhat related. This also explains the rise in performance between the Loupias-Laplace stable, and the Loupias-Laplace all detector. Regions where the scale selection mechanism fails and thus are neglected by the first detector are mainly uniform regions of the background. This also explains the comparatively good performance of the original Loupias detector with a fix scale. There, no areas are discarded. The usefulness of scale selection is demonstrated by the fact that for all numbers of detections, the results for the Loupias-Laplace all detector is better than with a fixed radius.

Overall, superior performance could be obtained by the Loupias-Laplace detector, even for a low number of detections. This shows that the Loupias-Laplace detector finds a variety of, yet not random, image structures beneficial for classification. Another advantage is that the number of detections can be adjusted in a straightforward way in order to obtain stable histograms.

2.4 Discussion

Interest point or region detection is an important step in many computer vision problems. We have given an overview about commonly used techniques for interest point detection as well as for scale selection. We have extended the wavelet based Loupias detector to deliver scale information, and evaluated the different detectors in terms of repeatability, clustering properties, type of structures detected, region coverage and classification performance.

Region detectors focus the attention to specific regions and thus reduce the data that has to be processed. They perform a kind of pre-filtering of the images. They narrow down the potential locations in the image to be analyzed. The precise description of the local structures is done in terms of features, as will be shown in the next chapter.

A reduction of image structures to be considered in the learning phase can also be achieved by labelling, e.g., by marking interesting object structures by hand. But then in the recognition stage, again the entire image has to be scanned for the desired structures. Moreover, the parts chosen by humans are not necessarily the best ones for machine based classification. Experiments performed by Viola and Jones (2001) show that for faces, e.g., the hair line is a stable feature, a part that is not likely to be chosen by humans. Manually selected parts are typically object dependant, and thus they cannot be shared between different object classes, as it is the case for general areas of interest. For huge image databases, fully automatic procedures are desirable for learning and recognition, so the development of reliable automatic region detectors is necessary.

The different interest point detectors react to different patterns in the image. Depending on the type of the object to be retrieved, the focus on a specific structure or a combination of different structure types is necessary. One solution is to use a combination of detectors responding to complementary patterns as proposed in Mikolajczyk and Schmid (2005), but at the cost of running multiple detectors. Another possibility is to use a detector responding to a greater variety of structures, here the Loupias-Laplace detector proved to be very successful. It is crucial that all important areas in an image are covered by interest regions, especially if the context is related to the object. Even random sampling can then be beneficial for object class recognition, since local detections are dispensed over the whole image. In this case though, since no selection of image structures is performed, a great number of interest points is necessary to represent the object.

The degree of distinctiveness of the detections directly influences the recognition strategy. When a variety of less discriminative structures is found, typically the distribution of these parts is considered, e.g., by histograms. In order to get a stable estimate of the distribution, a sufficient number of samples is required, and thus a sufficient number of detections. Geometry can still be accounted for, but again from a statistical point of view, e.g., in the form of co-occurrences Chapter 6 and 8 deals with these kind of classification strategies in more detail.

If we are able to construct very specific part detectors, we only need few detections. Then the occurrence of some parts alone can be an indicator for the presence of a particular object. Such specific part detectors might be special filters or convolution masks. For example, Reisert et al. (2007) have presented a method to detect specific structures by combinations of holomorphic filters, but these are only suitable for rather small patterns, like pollen porates with moderate intra class variations. On the very extreme end, we have a matched filter approach. These have the known disadvantages of being sensitive to distortions and other image transformations. We thus advocate the use of generic parts that can be used more flexibly.

3 Local Features

In this chapter, we want to introduce possible representations of the local areas, once they have been detected. Unless very specific filters have been used for detecting the regions, the detection itself does not characterize the local area sufficiently.

The focus of this work is the research of general algorithms using local representations for object classification, so the precise type of the description should be secondary. We therefore use a standard set of descriptors. We still present them here, since all following algorithms rely on these features. It is necessary to know what kind of information they cover. The reader familiar with the respective features may skip these sections.

3.1 Basic Notion

The creation of descriptions for the entities under consideration is a vital part of any pattern recognition system. These descriptions are referred to as *features* or *descriptors* and are typically interpreted as elements of some (multi dimensional) vector space χ, where the different dimensions constitute distinct types of observations. The term feature may refer to a single observation as well as to the entire n-tuple.

We will denote elements of such pattern spaces as bold face symbols, with the individual elements set in ordinary type, $\mathbf{x} = (x_1, \ldots, x_D)^\top \in \chi$. These spaces can be over any field $\mathbb{K}$, however, in this work, we only consider $\mathbb{K} = \mathbb{R}$, i.e. in our case $\chi = \mathbb{R}^D$.

In order to compare features, distance measures are used. If a distance measure $d : \chi \times \chi \to \mathbb{R}_+$ between $\mathbf{x}_1$ and $\mathbf{x}_2$ satisfies the following conditions, for all $\mathbf{x}_1, \mathbf{x}_2, \mathbf{x}_3 \in \chi$,

$$d(\mathbf{x}_1, \mathbf{x}_2) = d(\mathbf{x}_2, \mathbf{x}_1) \quad \text{(symmetry)}; \quad (3.1)$$
$$d(\mathbf{x}_1, \mathbf{x}_2) \geq 0 \quad \text{(positivity)}; \quad (3.2)$$
$$d(\mathbf{x}_1, \mathbf{x}_2) = 0, \text{ iff } \mathbf{x}_1 = \mathbf{x}_2; \quad (3.3)$$
$$d(\mathbf{x}_1, \mathbf{x}_3) \leq d(\mathbf{x}_1, \mathbf{x}_2) + d(\mathbf{x}_2, \mathbf{x}_3) \quad \text{(triangle inequality)}. \quad (3.4)$$

the distance is called a *metric*. A reasonable design of features assumes that their visual dissimilarity can be expressed as their distance in feature space. One possibility to measure the

3 Local Features

distance of two elements $\mathbf{x}_1$ and $\mathbf{x}_2$ is to calculate $\|\mathbf{x}_2 - \mathbf{x}_1\|$, i.e. the *norm* $\|.\| : \chi \to \mathbb{R}_+$ of the difference vector. A norm has to satisfy

$$\|\mathbf{x}\| \geq 0; \qquad (3.5)$$
$$\|\mathbf{x}\| = 0, \text{ iff } \mathbf{x} = \mathbf{0}; \qquad (3.6)$$
$$\|\lambda \mathbf{x}\| = |\lambda| \cdot \|\mathbf{x}\|, \qquad (3.7)$$
$$\|\mathbf{x}_1 + \mathbf{x}_2\| \leq \|\mathbf{x}_1\| + \|\mathbf{x}_2\|, \qquad (3.8)$$

for all $\mathbf{x}, \mathbf{x}_1, \mathbf{x}_2 \in \chi$ and $\lambda \in \mathbb{R}$. In order to compare features, several norms have been proposed. Some of the common norms are the $\mathbb{L}_p$ type norms,

$$\|\mathbf{x}\|_p = \left[\sum_{n=1}^{N} |x_n|^p\right]^{\frac{1}{p}}, \; p \geq 1 \qquad (3.9)$$

In particular, the $\mathbb{L}_2$ norm is referred to as *Euclidean* norm and used at different occasions throughout this work. It implicitly assumes that each dimension of the feature space is equally important. The $\mathbb{L}_1$-norm, also denoted as *city-block* distance or *Manhattan* distance is also used frequently.

Some elements of a feature vector might be correlated. When we have this knowledge in form of a covariance matrix $\mathbf{M}$, the *Mahalanobis* distance $d_M : \mathbb{R}^D \times \mathbb{R}^D \to \mathbb{R}_+$ can be used to take this knowledge into account. It was presented by Mahalanobis (1936) and is given by

$$d_M(\mathbf{x}_1, \mathbf{x}_2) = \sqrt{(\mathbf{x}_2 - \mathbf{x}_1)^\top \mathbf{M}^{-1} (\mathbf{x}_2 - \mathbf{x}_1)}. \qquad (3.10)$$

A commonly used similarity measure is the normalized cross correlation corr : $\mathbb{R}^D \times \mathbb{R}^D \to [-1, 1]$. It measures the similarity of two vectors based on their normalized inner product and is given by

$$\text{corr}(\mathbf{x}_1, \mathbf{x}_2) = \frac{\langle \mathbf{x}_1 - \mu_1, \mathbf{x}_2 - \mu_2 \rangle}{\|\mathbf{x}_1 - \mu_1\|_2 \|\mathbf{x}_2 - \mu_2\|_2}, \qquad (3.11)$$

where μ_1 and μ_2 are the mean values of the vector elements in $\mathbf{x}_1$ and $\mathbf{x}_2$ respectively, and $\langle .,. \rangle : \mathbb{R}^N \times \mathbb{R}^N \to \mathbb{R}$ is the Euklidean inner product. Normalized cross correlation has the nice property that it is invariant towards additional as well as multiplicative changes of the vectors. Please note that the normalized cross correlation is a similarity measure, and thus smaller values denote more dissimilar patterns, where as for distance measures, smaller values mean more similar patterns.

3.2 Feature Distributions

Whenever we want to describe a region or a whole image, it is useful to consider the distribution of the features contained in this area. This distribution can then be used as a descriptor for the entire region or the image.

Histograms are a discrete representation of a probability density function. Despite their simplicity, they have shown good performance in a variety of applications.

For histogram creation, a finite partition $\mathcal{X}$ of the space χ (in our case $\mathcal{X} \subset \chi$) is divided into N disjoint regions $\{\mathcal{X}_1, \ldots, \mathcal{X}_N\}$, following the rules:

$$\bigcup_{n=1}^{N} \mathcal{X}_n = \mathcal{X} \tag{3.12}$$

and

$$\mathcal{X}_n \cap \mathcal{X}_{n'} = \varnothing, \text{ if } n \neq n'. \tag{3.13}$$

These partitions are often referred to as *bins*. For traditional histograms, the feature space is partitioned into hypercubes of side length λ and volume $V = \lambda^D$. The bin centers $\mathbf{b}_n$, $n \in \{1, \ldots, N\}$ thus form an equally spaced grid. In a more general setting, the different dimensions could be partitioned using different λ_d, thus obtaining hypercuboids. In this case, the different dimensions have to be normalized separately. The volume is then calculated as $V = \prod_{d=1}^{D} \lambda_d$. However, this is not considered in the following, since the extension is straightforward and only clutters the notation. Given a set of samples $\mathbf{X} = \{\mathbf{x}_1, \ldots, \mathbf{x}_M\}$, $\mathbf{X} \subset \mathcal{X}$, their distribution can be estimated by the number of samples falling into the respective bins. For the estimation, a windowing function $f : \mathbb{R}^D \to \{0, 1\}$ determines which data entries are to be counted:

$$f(\mathbf{x}) = \begin{cases} 1 & \text{if all } |x_j| \leq \frac{1}{2},\ j \in \{1, \ldots, D\} \\ 0 & \text{otherwise} \end{cases}. \tag{3.14}$$

This function returns one if a point lies inside a unit cube centered at the origin, and zero otherwise. The histogram estimate $\hat{p}^H$ of some underlying density p of the data points is assumed to be constant inside a bin, i.e.

$$\hat{p}^H(\mathbf{x}) = \hat{p}(\mathbf{b}_n), \quad \forall \left\{ \mathbf{x} \Big| f\left(\frac{\mathbf{x} - \mathbf{b}_n}{\lambda}\right) = 1 \right\}. \tag{3.15}$$

3 Local Features

The estimation $\hat{p}$ of the density at a specific point in the feature space using a local window can be calculated as

$$\hat{p}(\mathbf{x}) = \frac{1}{V}\frac{1}{M}\sum_{i=1}^{M} f\left(\frac{\mathbf{x}_i - \mathbf{x}}{\lambda}\right). \tag{3.16}$$

The traditional histogram representation $\mathcal{H}(\mathbf{X})$ of a set of feature vectors $\mathbf{X}$ is an N-dimensional vector $(h_1, \ldots, h_N)^\top$ with the individual entries being $h_n = V\hat{p}(\mathbf{b}_n)$, with a windowing function as defined in equation (3.14). The normalization by the volume is neglected, since all bins have the same volume. The traditional histogram has a number of disadvantages, e.g., it is discontinuous at the bin boundaries and a large number of bins is needed to model a distribution accurately. By using a more sophisticated windowing functions (e.g. fuzzy voting, see Siggelkow (2002)), some of the disadvantages can be remedied. In a general setting, we are not restricted to regular grid points to evaluate equation (3.16). This becomes important when constructing local part histograms. This will be described in detail in chapter 7.

A common choice for comparing histograms is the *histogram intersection* measure. The histogram intersection $HI : \mathbb{R}_+^N \times \mathbb{R}_+^N \to \mathbb{R}_+$ of two vectors $\mathbf{x}_1$ and $\mathbf{x}_2$ is defined by

$$HI(\mathbf{x}_1, \mathbf{x}_2) = \sum_{n=1}^{N} \min(x_{1n}, x_{2n}). \tag{3.17}$$

When the vectors are normalized to represent probability distributions, i.e. $\sum_n^N x_n = 1$ and $x_n \geq 0, n \in \{1, \cdots, N\}$, then $0 \leq HI \leq 1$. In this case, histogram intersection is related to the $\mathbb{L}_1$ norm by

$$HI(\mathbf{x}_1, \mathbf{x}_2) = 1 - \frac{\|\mathbf{x}_1 - \mathbf{x}_2\|_1}{2}. \tag{3.18}$$

Like normalized cross correlation, histogram intersection is a similarity measure.

For discrete representations of probability distributions, also other similarity measures can be applied. The χ^2 test (see e.g. Fukunaga, 1990) motivated from statistics or the the Kullback-Leibler divergence (Kullback and Leibler, 1951) based on information theory are examples for such measures.

Besides histograms, also other forms to represent feature distributions exist. For example, Gaussian mixture models have shown to be suitable in an image retrieval setting using primitive features (Teynor et al., 2005). In this thesis, we solely rely on a histogram representation though.

3.3 Basic Feature Types

As a description of the pattern under consideration, the intensity values of the pixels can be vectorized and used. However, these features are sensitive towards illumination changes and noise. Furthermore, small shifts and/or rotations of the structure result in large differences of corresponding pixels and thus large distances in feature space. So more sophisticated techniques for feature construction have been proposed. The descriptions generated should be robust - in the ideal case invariant - against image transformations. A thorough treatment of the construction of invariant features can be found in Schulz-Mirbach (1995).

The use of powerful features has always been a crucial step in any pattern recognition system. In the context of CBIR or object classification, a huge variety of different features have been proposed. Evaluation papers like Mikolajczyk and Schmid (2005); Teynor et al. (2006) or Deselaers et al. (2008), have investigated the performance of diverse descriptions. As expected, different features are suitable for different tasks and objects. Since no single feature is able to distinguish between arbitrary classes, for general systems, the use of a variety of generic features is recommendable.

A suitable subset of this general pool of features can be identified by feature selection techniques. Relevant features might be found, by considering the inter- and intra-class variations of the features. This has been explored, e.g., by Setia and Burkhardt (2006). Another possibility for feature selection is to let the classifier itself decide which observations are relevant for distinguishing between classes. Here, the work by Opelt et al. (2006a), has to be mentioned in the context of visual object class recognition. They use boosting in order to determine capable descriptors. The Support Vector Machines (SVMs) (Schölkopf and Smola, 2001) as used in some of our experiments are able to implicitly perform feature selection on high dimensional data. Work by Ronneberger (2007) shows that SVMs are able to deal with feature vectors of 87,296 dimensions, and the cluster co-occurrence features presented later on in chapter 6 have 16,000 dimensions (see Setia et al., 2006a). Since we want to deal with generic object recognition, we follow this approach and use a variety of different descriptors, that have been proposed by different authors.

Some of the features presented in the next sections can either be calculated in a global, or a local context. Whenever a local region should be described, only the respective area as indicated by the interest point detector is used for feature computation.

In order to maintain invariance towards certain image transformations, for some features, it is necessary that the detected region is normalized, i.e. scaled to a reference size and/or rotated to a canonical orientation. Other feature extraction processes are invariant by themselves (see Schulz-Mirbach, 1995), and do not need such a normalization procedure.

3.3.1 Color Features

Color is an important aspect of human perception. Color features in form of color histograms have already been introduced by Swain and Ballard (1991) for image indexing and are still one of the most widely used basic descriptors for image content.

The color of an image pixel is represented in some color space, typically in RGB (Red, Green, Blue), where the different dimensions represent the relative intensity of light at a particular wave length. The different dimensions are referred to as *channels* in this context. The values for the three color channels range from zero meaning no light intensity, to one meaning maximum light intensity. For color histogram creation, the feature space $\mathcal{X} = [0, 1]^3$, is divided into N regions. A color histogram describes the fractions of pixels having color values that fall into the respective regions.

A property of a histogram is that all spatial coherence of the samples is neglected. A color histogram is thus not only invariant against rotations or translations of the object under consideration, but also against all possible pixel permutations. Nevertheless, it is still one of the most powerful color image descriptors (see evaluation in Deselaers et al., 2008).

Different color spaces have been introduced in the context of CBIR. The HSV (Hue, Saturation, Value) color space has been designed to be perceptually uniform (Wyszecki and Stiles, 1982) and is thus preferred over the RGB color space in this work.

A variety of other color based features, like color moments (Stricker and Orengo, 1995) or color correlograms (Huang et al., 1997) have also been proposed, but will not be used in this work.

3.3.2 Texture Features

Besides color, another important property of a region is its *texture*. The precise meaning of texture varies from author to author, no general definition has been agreed upon yet. Some authors like Tamura et al. (1978) or Gonzales and Woods (1993) describe properties like smoothness, coarseness or regularity of a structure by the term texture. Another commonly used notion of the term refers to a certain (repeated) geometric arrangement of image intensities. The IEEE Standard Glossary of Image Processing and Pattern Recognition Terminology refers to it as "[...], an attribute representing the spatial arrangement of the gray levels of the pixels in a region."

A great variety of texture description methods have been proposed, e.g. stochastic approaches like the co-occurrence matrices by Haralick et al. (1973), frequency domain based methods like Gabor (Turner, 1986) or wavelet filters (Sebe and Lew, 2000) and other methods like fractal descriptions (Keller et al., 1989), local binary patterns (Ojala et al., 2002), or the psycho-visually motivated Tamura texture features (Tamura et al., 1978), to just mention some of the most commonly used descriptors. As usual, the performance of the descriptors depends on the precise task at hand.

3.3 Basic Feature Types

In this work, we have chosen two basic kinds of texture descriptors, in particular the average energy of wavelet coefficients and invariant gray scale features with relational kernel functions as introduced in Schael and Burkhardt (1998). The wavelet energy features describe the degree of coarseness of a region and are thus consistent with Tamuras notion of texture. The invariant gray scale features with relational kernel functions have shown good performance in image retrieval applications (Siggelkow et al., 2001) and were thus selected.

Wavelet Coefficient based Roughness Measure

The wavelet coefficients as introduced in section 2.1.1, equation (2.10), code the degree of change in a signal at a respective wavelet decomposition level, and can thus serve as a measure of the coarseness of a particular region. Let $W_{2^{-j}}^D$ be the j-th subband in the D-direction, i.e. the image was filtered j times by the wavelet function ψ^D, $D \in \{HL, LH, HH\}$. Then the wavelet coefficient based roughness measure e for the area located at location x, y, scale s, at level j and direction D is given by

$$e_{D,j}(x,y,s) = \frac{1}{(2s^{-j}+1)^2} \sum_{k=\lfloor -s2^{-j} \rfloor}^{\lfloor s2^{-j} \rfloor} \sum_{\ell=\lfloor -s2^{-j} \rfloor}^{\lfloor s2^{-j} \rfloor} |W_{2^{-j}}^D(\lfloor x^{-j} \rfloor + k, \lfloor y^{-j} \rfloor + \ell)|. \quad (3.19)$$

Since we are dealing with a dyadic wavelet transform and a discrete image grid, the indices are subject to the floor function $\lfloor . \rfloor : \mathbb{R} \to \mathbb{Z}$.

The subbands $\{HL, LH, HH\}$ are treated separately, in order to get a description that incorporates the directional information. This yields three coefficients per decomposition stage j. When the descriptor should be robust against rotation, the three values can be summed:

$$e_j(x,y,s) = \frac{1}{3} \sum_D e_{D,j}(x,y,s) \quad (3.20)$$

The maximum number of decomposition stages to consider depends on the initial scale of the detection. In our experiments, we typically require a minimum radius of the detection of 5 pixels, thus three decomposition stages are chosen. Considering the three different directions separately, we obtain a 9-dimensional descriptor.

These features are of course a very rough description of the local texture, and are typically not sufficient on their own. However, they are useful for distinguishing between smooth and coarse regions. They have shown to increase the performance of classification when used together with other features, as e.g., color features.

In order to describe the precise structure of an area, more sophisticated features are necessary. We thus use relational gray scale features, which are described in the following.

3 Local Features

Relational Gray Scale Features

The relational gray scale features are motivated by the Local Binary Patterns (LBP) introduced by Ojala et al. (1996) for texture classification. In this work, they are used in chapter 8.

Local Binary Pattern features are invariant against monotonic gray scale transformations. They eliminate the effect of illumination by thresholding a neighborhood of pixels by its center pixel. Then the sign of the resulting values is considered instead of the value itself and mapped to the values 0 or 1 according to equation (3.22). Applying this to all pixels in a circular neighborhood of the center pixel, we obtain a binary pattern which can be transformed into a unique number by weighting the individual pattern locations by a power of 2 and summing the values, i.e.

$$LBP(\mathbf{x}) = \sum_{i=1}^{N} \Theta\left(I(\mathbf{z}_i^{\mathbf{x}}) - I(\mathbf{x})\right) 2^i, \qquad (3.21)$$

where

$$\Theta(x) = \begin{cases} 1 & \text{if } x \geq 0 \\ 0 & \text{if } x < 0 \end{cases} \qquad (3.22)$$

is the *unit step function* or *Heaviside function*. $\mathbf{Z}^{\mathbf{x}} = \{\mathbf{z}_1^{\mathbf{x}}, \cdots, \mathbf{z}_N^{\mathbf{x}}\}$ is a set of neighboring pixels for a center pixel $\mathbf{x} = (x, y)$. Since the signed difference $I(\mathbf{z}_i^{\mathbf{x}}) - I(\mathbf{x})$ is considered, the effect of gray scale shifts is totally eliminated. Invariance against scaling of the gray scale is achieved by the unit step function as the sign of the difference is mapped to 0 or 1 (Ojala et al., 2000).

It is obvious that the main disadvantage of these features is the discontinuity of the unit step function, which makes them sensitive to noise; a small disturbance in the image may cause a large deviation of the feature. To overcome this problem, Schael (2004) has introduced an operator which extends the step function in equation (3.22) to a ramp function

$$\text{rel}_\vartheta(x) = \begin{cases} 1 & \text{if } x < -\vartheta \\ \frac{\vartheta - x}{2\vartheta} & \text{if } -\vartheta \leq x \leq \vartheta \\ 0 & \text{if } \vartheta < x \end{cases}, \qquad (3.23)$$

where ϑ is a threshold parameter. Now function values in the range of $[0, 1]$ are possible. In this way, the features are much more robust against noise, but we also sacrifice complete invariance towards monotonic gray scale transformations. Robustness to these transformations can yet be preserved. If ϑ is set to zero, the rel function will reduce to $1 - \Theta$.

Based on the rel function defined in equation (3.23), a relational function $R : \mathbb{R} \times \mathbb{R} \times \mathbb{R}_+ \times \mathbb{R}_+ \times [0, 2\pi] \times \mathbb{N} \to \mathbb{R}^N$ can be defined. The parameters of this function are $\theta = \{x, y, r, r', \varphi, N\}$, where (x, y) are the coordinates where the feature should be centered. The two radii are denoted by r and r' and φ is the angle difference between sample points on the two circles. N is the

3.3 Basic Feature Types

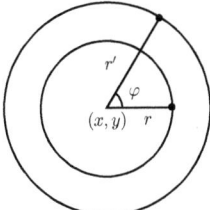

Figure 3.1: Visualization of the parameters for the relational function.

number of samples taken on each circle. The different parameters are illustrated in figure 3.1. The k-th element of the vectorial output of the function R is then given by

$$R(x,y,r,r',\varphi,N)_k = \mathrm{rel}_\vartheta(I(x_2,y_2) - I(x_1,y_1)), \qquad (3.24)$$

where
$$(x_1,y_1) = (x + r\cos(k \cdot 2\pi/N), y + r\sin(k \cdot 2\pi/N)) \qquad (3.25)$$

and
$$(x_2,y_2) = (x + r'\cos(k \cdot 2\pi/N + \varphi), y + r'\sin(k \cdot 2\pi/N + \varphi)). \qquad (3.26)$$

Bilinear interpolation is used for the evaluation of points not lying exactly on the image grid. Based on different combinations of r, r' and φ, local information at different scales and orientations can be captured. In order to be invariant towards scale changes, the radii r and r' can be normalized by the scale factor of the detection. To obtain rotation invariance, the different entries of the vector can be summed, as explained in Schael (2004), based on the principle of constructing invariant features by Haar integration.

3.3.3 Shape Features

The third category of features used in this thesis is concerned with the *shape* of a local area. Shape in this context means a distinct surface structure as opposed to texture, which typically requires some repetition inside a region. We do not use shape features which deal with the contour or the outline of an object, since these approaches rely on segmentation, which we deliberately want to avoid. Shape features should capture object characteristics like edges, corners, and the distinct structure of certain areas.

A very prominent example for local shape features are the SIFT features by Lowe (2004). They are weighted localized gradient direction histograms. A variety of modified versions have been proposed. The GLOH (Gradient Location Orientation Histogram) features by Mikolajczyk and Schmid (2005), e.g., use a polar instead of a rectangular coordinate system. The PCA-SIFT

3 Local Features

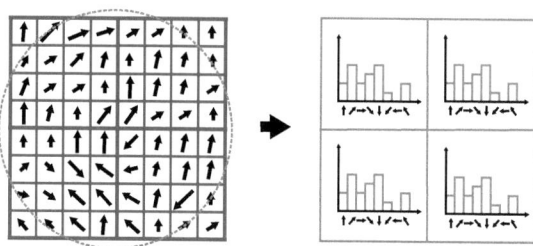

Figure 3.2: Construction of the SIFT descriptor. Histograms for localized gradient directions are constructed, by summing the Gaussian weighted gradient magnitudes of pixels falling inside the respective regions.

features by Ke and Sukthankar (2004) do not use histograms of the gradient directions, but the gradients of the entire region are vectorized and subject to a Principal Component Analysis (PCA).

SIFT as well as GLOH features were used in some of our experiments, in particular in sections 4.3, 5.3 and 9.1.3. In the following, we want to introduce the SIFT descriptor as the main representative for this class of features. For the image area under consideration, the gradient magnitudes and orientations are computed. They are sampled according to a local grid. The size of the grid depends on the desired number of local regions and how many sample points should be used inside a region. The grid is adapted to the scale of the local detection. Lowe proposed to consider 4×4 regions, and for each region, to take 4×4 samples. For each region, the angles of the gradients are quantized into 8 directions. Thus, a SIFT descriptor has $4 \times 4 \times 8 = 128$ elements. For constructing the local histograms, the gradient magnitude of each sample location is used, weighted by a Gaussian window centered at the origin of the detection. The scale of the Gaussian is half of the scale of the local detection. This is done to weigh the locations with a large distance to the initial detection less, since they are affected by misregistration errors more severely. In order to obtain rotation invariance, the gradient main direction of the local area gets calculated and all gradient directions measured according to this base direction.

The process is visualized in figure 3.2. On the left, a grid with 2×2 spatial locations is shown (instead of the original 4×4 grid, due to space reasons). For each local sub-area, the image is sampled at 4×4 locations. The gradient magnitude and the gradient direction are visualized as the length and the direction of the arrows. The gradient magnitudes are weighted by a Gaussian window. Now for each local sub-area, a histogram of gradient directions is created, which can be seen on the right in figure 3.2. The entries for the histograms are concatenated and the final feature vector obtained.

3.4 Combining Features

As described above, typically no single feature is able to capture all characteristics of a local area alone. Thus for some applications, it is useful to combine several complementary descriptors. This has been performed, e.g., for the classification of animal images for the MUSCLE project (see the experiments in section 2.3.3) and has obtained superior results compared to the individual features alone. To create a combined feature vector for a specific local region, the different kinds of features $\{\mathbf{x}_1, \ldots, \mathbf{x}_N\}$ extracted from this area are just concatenated, $\tilde{\mathbf{x}} = (\mathbf{x}_1^\top, \ldots, \mathbf{x}_N^\top)^\top$. The resulting feature vector $\tilde{\mathbf{x}}$ lives in a larger dimensional space. Let $\dim(\mathbf{x}_i)$ denote the dimensionality of the vector $\mathbf{x}_i$, then $\tilde{\mathbf{x}} \in \mathbb{R}^{\sum_{i=1}^N \dim(\mathbf{x}_i)}$.

Distance measures as introduced in section 3.1 typically weigh each dimension equally, so the values of the concatenated feature vectors have to be in the same range, otherwise features with large ranges might dominate the result. Typically, the values are rescaled to the range $[0, 1]$ (Aksoy and Haralick, 2002).

Different normalization strategies can be applied, we will present only the most commonly used, i.e. linear scaling to unit range, linear scaling to unit variance and transformation to a uniform random variable.

Linear scaling to unit range:
Let x be a feature component. ℓ and u are the lower and upper bounds of the feature's value, respectively. ℓ and u can either be determined theoretically or may be inquired from a sample database. Then

$$x' = \frac{x - \ell}{u - \ell} \qquad (3.27)$$

is the normalized feature.

Linear scaling to unit variance:
Here, the feature value gets normalized to a random variable with zero mean and unit variance as

$$x' = \frac{x - \mu}{\sigma} \qquad (3.28)$$

with μ denoting the mean and σ the standard deviation of the feature values.

Transformation to a uniform random variable:
Given a cumulative distribution function $F(x)$, a feature can be transformed via

$$x' = F(x) \qquad (3.29)$$

and will then be uniformly distributed in the range $[0, 1]$ (Papoulis and Pillai, 2002).

Aksoy and Haralick (2002) have evaluated several feature normalization methods for image retrieval applications. They reported that normalization methods according to the feature distribution typically yield better performance than simple linear scaling to unit range, in particular the transformation to a uniform random variable.

3.5 Discussion

A variety of features have been proposed for CBIR and object classification. In this chapter, we have introduced the basic understanding of features as elements of some high dimensional vector space, where the (dis-)similarity can be measured by some distance function.

In this work, we did not attempt a complete evaluation of all possible features for object classification or to develop a new set of descriptors. Since we focus on general techniques using local representations for object classification, we have used a representative set of standard features. The different descriptors used in this work show that the approaches presented in this thesis are general enough to work with a large range of conceptually different features.

4 Visual Codebooks

Once regions of interest have been found in images and features have been calculated from these areas, they can be used for recognition. Typically, these local features are not used directly for learning. As an intermediate level of abstraction, *visual codebooks* are introduced. A variety of different algorithms rely on visual codebooks at some step in the recognition chain, e.g., Agarwal and Roth (2002); Fei-Fei et al. (2006); Mikolajczyk et al. (2006) or Opelt et al. (2006b), just to mention a few.

A general codebook $\mathbf{C}$ is a set of vectors distributed in some feature space χ

$$\mathbf{C} = \{\mathbf{c}_i | \mathbf{c}_i \in \chi, i = \{1, \ldots, K\}\}. \tag{4.1}$$

In a codebook, representative visual structures are collected that can serve as a vocabulary for later processing stages. In particular, the codebooks can be used to label new feature vectors by assigning the number of the closest codebook entry to them (see section 8). Another application for codebooks is model construction: certain object properties, i.e. the geometrical relation of parts, has only to be determined for a limited number of structures.

The main reason for the use of codebooks is to be able to deal with the huge number of high dimensional features obtained from the images. For a typical multi class object recognition problem, hundreds of thousands of different local representations might be extracted from the training and test images. This is too much to be handled directly by most algorithms. A common solution to the problem is to apply clustering techniques to the features extracted from the training images. For each cluster, a single representative is chosen and thus the number of different structures to be considered is reduced.

The goal of codebook creation in our context is to define a suitable partition of the high dimensional feature spaces. In order to find representative structures that can serve as codebook entries, we would like to focus on dense regions in feature space, i.e. regions where common structures occur. A typical feature vector used for a local description consists of 128 dimensions, e.g., the SIFT descriptor (Lowe, 2004) or the GLOH descriptor (Mikolajczyk et al., 2005a). Precise density estimation in this 128-dimensional space is prohibitive, since on one hand, we would need an enormous mass of data, and on the other hand, the representation of this density would be very difficult. If we would choose, e.g., an unparametric representation in form of a histogram with each dimension quantized into 4 bins, we would end up with a $4^{128} \approx 1.2 \cdot 10^{77}$ dimensional vector, which is almost as much as the estimated number of atoms in the universe ($\approx 10^{80}$).

4 Visual Codebooks

In this chapter, we present a novel approach to obtain visual codebooks by identifying sufficiently dense regions in feature space given a desired similarity threshold. The algorithm identifies feature clusters with low variance. The method is much faster than other commonly used clustering algorithms as K-means or agglomerative clustering and can therefore be used to process more local features.

4.1 Related Work

A variety of different clustering algorithms have been applied to visual codebook creation, e.g. hierarchical clustering (divisive clustering (Linde et al., 1980) as well as agglomerative clustering), clustering based on function optimization (e.g. expectation maximization type clustering), density based clustering (Jurie and Triggs, 2005) or mixed techniques (Leibe et al., 2006). A general overview about clustering algorithms can be found in Theodoridis and Koutroumbas (2006). The two most commonly used techniques for codebook generation are agglomerative hierarchical clustering as well as K-means clustering. We review them briefly here. The task is to cluster a set of local appearance features $\mathbf{X} = \{\mathbf{a}_1, \ldots, \mathbf{a}_N\}$, $\mathbf{a}_i \in \chi$, and to obtain a codebook $\mathbf{C}$ as defined in equation (4.1).

Agglomerative hierarchical clustering

In the beginning, all data entries are regarded as single clusters. In each subsequent step, the most similar clusters are grouped, until only a single cluster remains. In this way, a tree structure of the data is created. To obtain the final partition, the tree is cut, either according to the desired number of clusters or a given minimum similarity between clusters. In order to determine the similarity between clusters, different strategies can be applied. They are referred to as *linkage strategies*. Typically, the average link paradigm is used as it produces compact clusters, although it has a rather high time ($O(N^2 \log(N))$) and space complexity ($O(N^2)$). This method is, e.g., applied by Agarwal et al. (2004) or Leibe et al. (2004) for codebook creation.

K-means clustering

K-means clustering is an iterative procedure, where a function J describing the within-cluster variance gets minimized:

$$J(\mathbf{X}) = \sum_{j=1}^{K} \sum_{i=1}^{N_j} d(\mathbf{a}_{ij}, \boldsymbol{\mu}_j). \qquad (4.2)$$

We have K clusters, each consisting of N_j members, $\boldsymbol{\mu}_j$ is the cluster mean of cluster j and d is a distance function. The time complexity of this algorithm is $O(NKq)$, where q is the number of iterations needed. The main advantage of K-means clustering is its simplicity, however, it is sensitive to outliers. The number of clusters has to be fixed a priori, and the cluster means might lie far away from the cluster members. When random initialization is used, the clustering result might differ between runs. In the context of codebook generation, K-means clustering is used, e.g., by Weber et al. (2000) or Lazebnik et al. (2006).

4.2 Sequential Clustering

4.2.1 Clustering Algorithm

Our goal is to find a partitioning of a high dimensional feature space for part based object class recognition. Typical clustering algorithms as described in the previous section do in fact more than that. They try to recover the structure of the data in feature space, e.g. by building a tree or minimizing an error criterion. For common objective functions, as in equation (4.2), this results in a higher number of cluster centers in more densely populated regions in feature space than in sparsely populated regions.

If we follow the principle of Occam's razor, we should select the simplest method that solves our problem. We only need to identify "sufficiently dense" regions in feature space and distribute cluster centers in these areas in order to get representative structures. We propose a simple sequential algorithm with low runtime complexity. The basic idea is to create hyper-spheres with a certain radius. As all clustering algorithms, we assume that the distance in feature space does resemble the visual similarity of the patches. So the radius to be chosen depends on the distance in which samples are still considered visually similar. This has to be done experimentally. A method how this can be accomplished is described in section 4.2.2.

The proposed algorithm is based on the Modified Basic Sequential Algorithmic Scheme (MB-SAS) as described in Theodoridis and Koutroumbas (2006). It is a two pass algorithm where first candidate cluster centers are determined. Then, the data is assigned to the respectively closest cluster centers. After all data has been assigned, new cluster representatives are calculated from the cluster members in order to represent them better. Clusters with too few members get discarded. The algorithmic description can be found in algorithm 4.1.

A difference of our algorithm to the original algorithm described in Theodoridis and Koutroumbas (2006) is that the cluster centers are calculated after the assignment of all members, and only if the minimum member constraint has been fulfilled. This further speeds up computation. The result of the clustering algorithm will depend on the order of the input. To not bias the result, the features should not be fed to the algorithm in the order they were extracted from the images, but shuffled beforehand. In order to determine the cluster representative, different methods are possible. In this work, the mean vector of the cluster members is taken.

The time complexity of MBSAS is $O(NK)$, which is smaller than the complexity of agglomerative or K-means clustering. Please note that for calculating the time complexity, K is the initial number of candidate clusters generated in the first part of the algorithm, not the final number of valid clusters. How significant the speed up is can be seen from the actual clustering times for sample datasets in section 4.3.3.

4 Visual Codebooks

Algorithm 4.1: Modified Sequential Clustering for Codebook Generation

Input: appearance features $\mathbf{X} = \{\mathbf{a}_1, \ldots, \mathbf{a}_N\}$; hyper-sphere radius ε; min density θ ;
Output: visual codebook $\mathbf{C} = \{\mathbf{c}_1, \ldots, \mathbf{c}_K\}$;
begin
    $m \longleftarrow 1$;
    $\mathbf{c}'_m \longleftarrow \mathbf{a}_1$;
    // search for cluster candidates $\mathbf{c}'$
    for $i \longleftarrow 2$ **to** N **do**
        Find $k \longleftarrow \arg\min_{1 \leq j \leq m} d(\mathbf{a}_i, \mathbf{c}'_j)$;
        if $d(\mathbf{a}_i, \mathbf{c}'_k) > \varepsilon$ **then**
            $m \longleftarrow m + 1$;
            $\mathbf{c}'_m \longleftarrow \mathbf{a}_i$;
        end
    end
    // assign data to cluster candidates
    for $i \longleftarrow 1$ **to** N **do**
        Find $\ell \longleftarrow \arg\min_{1 \leq j \leq m} d(\mathbf{a}_i, \mathbf{c}'_j)$;
        $\mathbf{C}^\ell \longleftarrow \mathbf{C}^\ell \cup \{\mathbf{a}_i\}$;
    end
    // select valid clusters, assign cluster representative
    $k \longleftarrow 0$;
    for $i \longleftarrow 1$ **to** m **do**
        if $|\mathbf{C}^i| \geq \theta$ **then**
            $k \longleftarrow k + 1$;
            $\mathbf{c}_k \longleftarrow$ getClusterRepresentative$(\mathbf{C}^i)$;
            $\mathbf{C} \longleftarrow \mathbf{C} \cup \{\mathbf{c}_k\}$;
        end
    end
end

4.2.2 Determining the Similarity Threshold

For the selection of a suitable hypershere radius ε for the MBSAS clustering algorithm, it is necessary to determine a threshold in feature space that indicates that two local areas are considered to be visually similar. We determined this threshold experimentally in a user experiment. Pairs of local detections were shown to different individuals who had to judge their visual similarity. The options were: "very similar" (++), "similar" (+), "not sure" (o), "dissimilar"(-) or "very dissimilar"(- -). The setup of the user interface can be seen from figure 4.1.

The local detections were displayed side by side. We used areas detected by the Hessian-Laplace detector, extracted from images of the Caltech 101 database. Since we used GLOH features for comparing the structures which only consider gray-scale information, the local parts were

4.2 Sequential Clustering

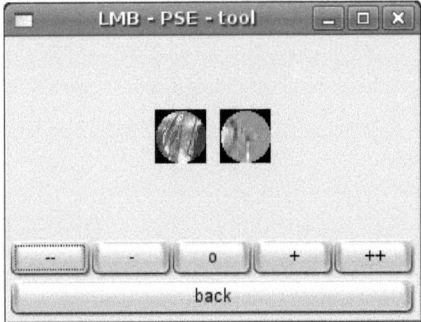

Figure 4.1: User interface for evaluating the visual distance of local parts.

displayed as intensity images.

Seven users participated in our experiment. Everyone judged 500 pairs of local structures. Every participant received identical judgement guidelines for the task, since the instruction "judge the similarity" can be interpreted in very different respects. The guidelines given were dependent on the type of features used later on, i.e., shape features (rotation sensitive GLOH features). Even after describing the desired type of similarity, there were still variations in the interpretation of the task by the individual subjects. The instructions given to the subjects can be read in the following:

```
Judgement guidelines:
---------------------

* The texture/structure/structural layout of the patches
  should be evaluated. No color information is given.

* The patches are shown at their original size. The scale
  of the patches themselves does not matter, but the scale
  of the structure contained in them (relative to the
  bounding circle).

* The orientation of the patches does matter (no rotation
  invariance, but a little robustness might not harm...).

* If you are not sure about the similarity of a pair, rather
  click  o = "not sure", than "not similar at all".
```

4 Visual Codebooks

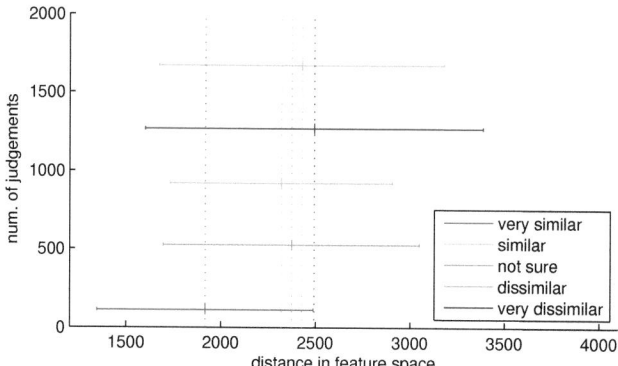

Figure 4.2: Average distance of local detections in GLOH feature space. For each group (pairs judged to be "very similar", "similar", "not sure", "dissimilar" and "very dissimilar", the mean (dotted) and the standard deviation (solid) of the calculated distance in feature space is displayed in respect to the number of judgements for each group.

For each structure judged, a GLOH feature vector was created. We wanted to infer whether the distances in features space do resemble the visual impression observed by the users. We calculated the mean value and the standard deviation of the Euclidean distances in GLOH feature space for pairs of local detections that were judged to belong to the same group (either "very similar", "similar","not sure","dissimilar" or "very dissimilar").

These values are displayed with respect to the number of judgements for each group in figure 4.2. From the result plot, we can see that the GLOH features in general are suitable for describing shape similarity, since the mean distances for the groups are in the right relative order: the group of very similar structures has on average the smallest Euclidean distance, getting gradually larger for the "similar" and the "not sure" group. The "very dissimilar" group has on average the largest values. Comparatively few pairs were judged to be be similar, the majority of pairs were judged to be either "dissimilar" or "very dissimilar". When pairs were judged to be "very similar" the average Euclidean distance was significantly smaller than the values for the other groups.

We can also observe that the variances of the judgements are quite large. This might be due to several reasons. First, the visual appearance of the individual parts is judged differently by different subjects, and secondly, the distance in feature space does not necessarily have to correspond to the perceived visual distance by humans. For color, much effort has been spent to design feature spaces, where the visual distance corresponds to the distance in feature space. The international committee on colorimetry (Commission Internationale de l'Eclairage, CIE) developed a series of color spaces that should be perceptually uniform, i.e. the CIE 1976 (L*, u*, v*) and the CIE 1976 (L*, a*, b*) color space (Wyszecki and Stiles (1982)). Also the HSV color space is approximately perceptual uniform. For texture and shape features, the development of such features spaces is difficult, since their dimensionality is typically much higher and the visual stimulus much more complex. A more thorough investigation of the correlation between the perceptual similarity of local image structure (or texture) and feature distances would be a worthwhile research topic on its own.

Once judgements for a certain type of visual similarity (structure, texture, color, etc.) exist, the user experiments do not have to be repeated for new features belonging to that class. The judgements can be reused. The new features just have to be computed for the local areas used in the evaluation and the distances can be determined accordingly.

For the following experiments, the hypershpere radius ε for the MBSAS-clustering was set in between the average Euclidean distance in feature space for the groups "very similar" and "similar".

4.3 Experimental Evaluation

To evaluate the performance of our new codebook generation algorithm in comparison to the standard agglomerative and K-means clustering algorithms, we conducted several experiments. We used two different databases, each with a different classification task. One dataset is the Caltech3[1] dataset (airplanes, faces, motorbikes together with a distinct background class), the other is the Caltech101 dataset[2], a collection of 101 diverse image categories.

For each image in the respective database, we extracted Harris-Laplace as well as Hessian-Laplace interest points (Mikolajczyk and Schmid, 2004). As explained in chapter 2, the Harris-Laplace detector fires on corners, where the Hessian-Laplace detector finds blob-like structures. The two types of interest points were treated separately in order to verify that the qualitative results do not depend on the type of interest point detector used. For each region, we calculated rotation sensitive GLOH (Mikolajczyk et al., 2005a) descriptors. For the computations, the programs provided by Mikolajczyk were used[3].

From each database, 30,000 local features were drawn randomly from the training images and clustered with the MBSAS, K-means and agglomerative clustering scheme. This number was mainly limited by the time complexity of the agglomerative clustering algorithm. For the Caltech101 database, we used 15 randomly selected training and test images. We drew three independent sets and averaged the respective results. For the Caltech3 database, the same training and test images were used as in Fergus et al. (2003), in order to be comparable with their results.

[1] from http://www.robots.ox.ac.uk/~vgg/data3.html
[2] from http://www.vision.caltech.edu/Image_Datasets/Caltech101
[3] from http://www.robots.ox.ac.uk/~vgg/research/affine/

4 Visual Codebooks

We discarded single member clusters for all clustering results, since they are considered as too uncommon to generalize well. So we set $\theta = 2$ in our case. In order to have comparable codebook sizes, the cut value for the agglomerative clustering was chosen such that after the removal of the single member clusters the number of clusters is the same as for the MBSAS clustering. The initial number of clusters for the K-means clustering was set so that the resulting number of non single member clusters was as close as possible to the value of the two other approaches. Since our K-means algorithm uses random initialization, it is hard to obtain exactly the same number.

4.3.1 Codebook Statistics

We first wanted to look at certain statistics of the different kinds of codebooks generated. We analyzed the number of clusters obtained after the removal of the single member clusters as well as the single cluster ratio (scr), i.e. the percentage of the clusters that contained just a single member. For each cluster, we computed the cluster variance, i.e. the average squared distance of the cluster members to the cluster center. We list the average cluster variance per codebook and also the distribution of the cluster variances. The results can be seen from table 4.1 for the Caltech3 database, and from table 4.2 for the Caltech101 database.

The results are very consistent across the different databases and interest point detector types. The clustering with MBSAS results in visually very compact clusters, with a low average cluster variance. As can be seen from the distribution of the variances of the clusters, there are no clusters with a very big variance, as e.g., for the K-means clusters. Cluster centers obtained as an average from widely spread data points are not guaranteed to represent the members adequately. This can also be confirmed by visual inspection of the clusters: patches belonging to some K-means clusters are visually quite distinct. As a consequence, the single cluster ratio is comparatively high for MBSAS codebooks as opposed to the other approaches, since only areas with a certain part density in a small neighborhood are kept.

4.3.2 Classification Results

In order to compare the codebooks from a qualitative point of view, we performed two classification tasks. We first solve a two class problem on the Caltech3 database, where objects have to be distinguished from a background class. We then deal with a multi class problem on the Caltech101 database.

Besides the properties of the different clustering algorithms, we are also interested in the performance of different methods how to assign newly extracted features to codebook entries. We have tested two commonly used approaches, i.e. nearest neighbor matching and threshold based matching. We also applied a weighted matching scheme based on the sigmoid function, which we found very suitable.

4.3 Experimental Evaluation

	Hessian-Laplace		
	MBSAS	Agg.	K-means
# of clusters	5489	5489	5005
scr	0.71	0.40	0.33
avg. var.	$0.94 \cdot 10^6$	$1.76 \cdot 10^6$	$2.42 \cdot 10^6$
var. distr.			

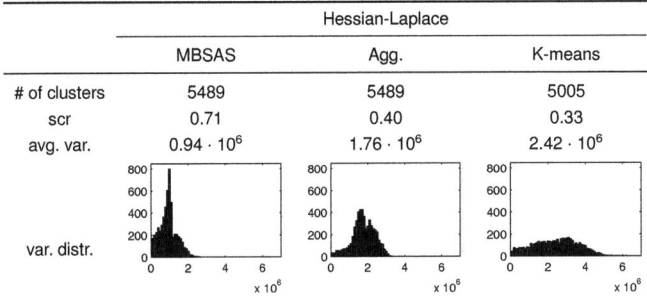

	Harris-Laplace		
	MBSAS	Agg.	K-means
# of clusters	5817	5817	5540
scr	0.69	0.39	0.26
avg. var.	$0.83 \cdot 10^6$	$1.65 \cdot 10^6$	$2.37 \cdot 10^6$
var. distr.			

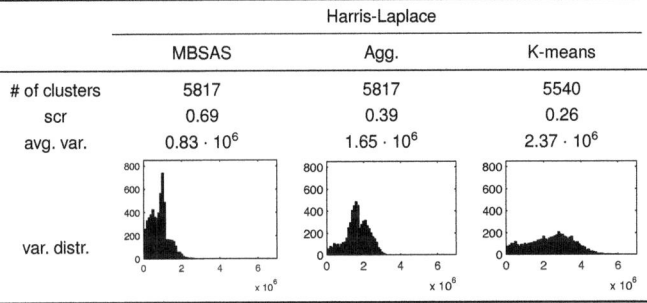

Table 4.1: Cluster statistics for codebooks for the Caltech3 database: scr = single cluster ratio, avg. var. = average variance, var. dist. = variance distribution.

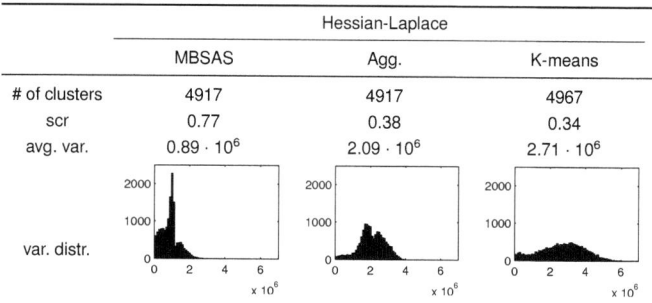

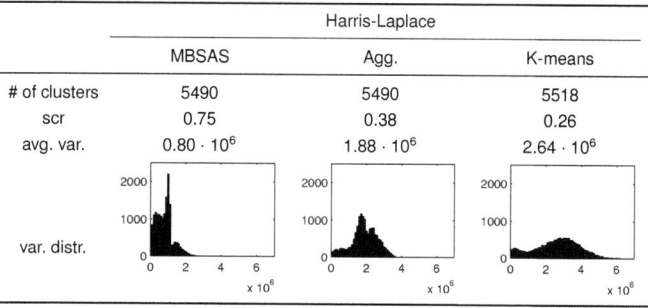

Table 4.2: Cluster statistics for codebooks for the Caltech101 database: scr = single cluster ratio, avg. var. = average variance, var. dist. = variance distribution.

4.3 Experimental Evaluation

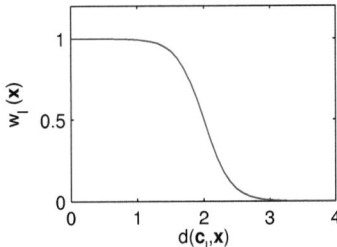

Figure 4.3: Sample sigmoid function with $\alpha = 5$ and $\varepsilon = 2$.

N nearest neighbor matching: The feature vector gets matched to the n nearest cluster centers, no matter what the distance is. We use $n = 3$ in our experiments.

Threshold based matching: The features match to all cluster centers that are within a certain threshold. The threshold is the hyper-sphere radius used for clustering. Thus, a vector might match to zero, one or more clusters.

Weighted matching using a sigmoid function: A new feature vector x matches to a codebook entry c_k with the weight $w_{c_k} : \mathbb{R}^{\dim(\mathcal{X})} \to [0, 1]$ determined by a sigmoid function

$$w_{c_k}(\mathbf{a}) = \frac{1}{1 + e^{\alpha(d(\mathbf{c}_k, \mathbf{a}) - \varepsilon)}}. \quad (4.3)$$

w_{c_k} can also be seen as a window function around the cluster center of c_k. The rationale behind this assignment function is that within a certain radius ε, the patches are all visually similar and should get the same high matching score. Patches with a distance above a threshold are too dissimilar and should get a low matching score. The region in between can be modelled by the factor α. It determines how steep the sigmoid function is. A sample sigmoid function can be seen from figure 4.3.

For histogram creation, the matching values for each feature get normalized to sum up to one, i.e. each feature contributes the same to the distribution.

Since we want to test the quality of the codebooks obtained, we use a simple bag-of-features approach as described in section 7: we create histograms of object parts using the different codebooks and matching strategies. We neglect any spatial information. For classification, we use a standard SVM implementation (libSVMTL[4]) with a histogram intersection kernel. For the multi class problem, a one-vs-rest SVM is used.

The two class problem on the Caltech3 database is comparatively easy as the images contain distinct structures for the individual object classes. Caltech101 is more diverse and contains a

---
[4]http://lmb.informatik.uni-freiburg.de/lmbsoft/libsvmtl/

4 Visual Codebooks

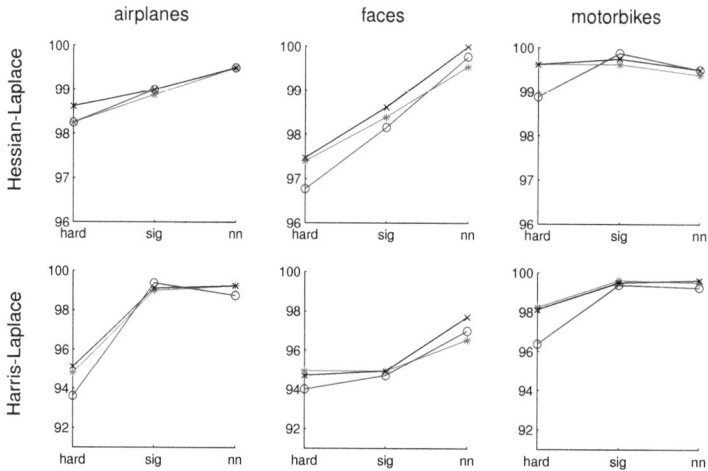

Table 4.3: Classification rate in % for the different Caltech3 problems. Results for MBSAS codebooks are shown in blue (o), for agglomerative codebooks in red (*) and for K-means codebooks in black (x). The results are given for the different matching strategies: hard = hard, sig = sigmoid and nn = 3 nearest neighbor.

variety of different structures. The classification results for the different interest point detector types and matching strategies can be seen from table 4.3 for the Caltech3 database and from table 4.4 for the Caltech101 database.

The overall classification performance for the Caltech3 database is very well, in particular we could obtain a classification rate of 100% for the faces class with Hessian-Laplace interest points and K-means clustering. In general, Hessian-Laplace interest points performed better than the Harris-Laplace interest points. For the Caltech101 database, more sophisticated classification strategies incorporating also spatial information have shown to obtain better results (see e.g. Lazebnik et al. (2006)). However, in this work we want to compare the relative performance of different clustering schemes, and thus we chose this basic setting.

From a classification point of view, there is no best clustering scheme. For the Caltech3 database and sigmoid matching, the MBSAS codebooks are slightly superior compared to the others regarding the categories airplanes and motorbikes. For the faces category, K-means clustering is superior when using nearest neighbor matching. Agglomerative clustering gives best results for the Caltech101 database and sigmoid matching.

4.3 Experimental Evaluation

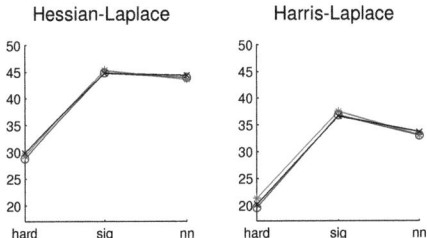

Table 4.4: Classification rate in % for the Caltech101 problem. Results for MBSAS codebooks are shown in blue (o), for agglomerative codebooks in red (*) and for K-means codebooks in black (x). The results are given for the different matching strategies: hard = hard matching, sig = sigmoid matching and nn = 3 nearest neighbor matching.

Using hard matching with a tight threshold typically gives inferior results compared to using sigmoid or nearest neighbor matching. Here the MBSAS clusters are especially sensitive. When the structures are distinct as in the Caltech3 database, nearest neighbor matching is superior in almost all cases, since the nearest parts matched are likely to be from the same class. For more diverse databases as the Caltech101 database, sigmoid matching performed best.

4.3.3 Run-times

In this section, we list experimental run-times for the different approaches. We performed the clustering for a different number of GLOH features computed around Hessian-Laplace interest points extracted from the Caltech101 dataset. The processing times were measured on 2.6 GHz AMD opteron processors. The results are listed in table 4.5.

For the agglomerative and the K-means clustering, we used the C clustering library by de Hoon et al. (2004). In this implementation, the K-means algorithm iterates until the assignment of features to clusters does not change any more. The MBSAS implementation was done by ourselves. The run times for the agglomerative clustering represent the time the entire tree needs for building, the run times for K-means and MBSAS clustering are given for settings that result in about the same number of clusters. For larger amounts of data, we increased the required number of members for clusters to be valid.

We can observe that the processing time for K-means and MBSAS clustering grows over-proportional to the number of features. This is due to the fact that for the K-means algorithm, the number of iterations (q) until convergence is larger, and for the MBSAS algorithm, the number of candidate clusters in the first part of the algorithm is larger.

4 Visual Codebooks

# of local features	10^4	$3 \cdot 10^4$	10^5	$5 \cdot 10^5$
# of clusters	~750 ($\theta = 2$)	~3000 ($\theta = 2$)	~3700 ($\theta = 4$)	~5000 ($\theta = 10$)
Agg. clustering	26.6 min	11.6 h	n.a.	n.a.
K-means clustering	15.3 min	4.0 h	36.3 h	n.a.
MBSAS clustering	1.9 min	16.7 min	2.0 h	45.6 h

Table 4.5: Experimental run-time results for different numbers of local features and clustering schemes.

The MBSAS algorithm runs very fast compared to the other algorithms. Thus it is possible to use more local representations in order to get a more complete view on the data. When increasing the hyper-sphere radius ε in which structures are considered similar, an even larger speed up is possible.

4.4 Discussion

The use of visual codebooks is a necessary part in many object classification and localization systems. In this chapter we have analyzed established schemes for codebook generation, and we presented a novel scheme how to obtain codebooks. Our experiments have shown that the different methods result in codebooks with different properties of the resulting clusters. In particular, the average cluster variance, the distribution of the cluster variances and the single cluster ratio can be different. Still all three approaches performed similarly in a bag-of-feature classification approach.

It seems to be sufficient to have cluster centers distributed in approximately the right area of the feature space. Following the principle of Occam's razor, we have shown that no complicated algorithms with huge memory and run-time requirements are necessary, a simple sequential clustering scheme is sufficient. So a large amount of local structures can be used in codebook generation, to get a more thorough view on the distribution of the data.

In the course of the work, it became apparent that the matching scheme has more influence on the recognition performance than the clustering algorithm: for diverse structures, sigmoid matching has shown to be superior, but also simple nearest neighbor matching is well suited, especially for simple problems.

5 Semantic Codebooks

In the previous chapter, we have shown how to create codebooks of visually similar structures for object class recognition. However, a specific object part might have different appearances. Treating these visually distinct, but semantically equivalent structures separately may be harmful for part based object class models. In this chapter, we discuss this problem and present a method how to group semantic parts.

A visualization of the problem can be found in figure 5.1. There, different visual representations of the letter "A" are depicted. Visual features extracted from each of these letters would be quite distinct. It is important to remember that we deal with a single *semantic* class here, however, with a variety of *visual* classes. Searching for a single visual representation for the semantic class "A" is not sufficient.

Figure 5.1: Visually different structures having the same semantic meaning (image according to Hofstadter (1986)).

The variety in the visual appearance of semantically equal object parts might be due to several reasons. First, there are natural intra class variabilities, e.g., engine parts of a motorbike that look different. Then, we also have to deal with different poses, e.g. a mouth might be open, shut, or smiling showing the teeth. But also other reasons exist: current feature extraction methods often rely on interest point detections. However, they are not always on the same locations on different object instances. This might result in shifted local windows for the same object part. So an eye might not always occur at the center of a local window, but also slightly shifted to the left or right. The features extracted from such shifted windows can be fairly different. Invariance towards such shifts might be incorporated into the local features, but it has been shown that whenever the user selects a too high degree of invariance, the recognition performance for object categories can be degraded. For example, the letters "6" and "9" can not be distinguished any more using rotation invariant descriptors. Some very successful features like the SIFT features or the GLOH features deliberately do not only consider the frequency of certain structures, but also their location. These types of features are affected by shifts in the detected structure.

5 Semantic Codebooks

A separate treatment of semantically similar parts might be critical when using bag-of-feature approaches. Parts with the same role might be matched to different dictionary entries. Distance calculation between part histograms are typically performed in a bin-by-bin fashion, so performance can be degraded by not relating semantically similar parts. Although cross bin measures have been developed, they rely on a ground distance between individual bins, which cannot be established easily for the semantic closeness of object structures.

In this chapter, we present a novel way how to perform a semantic grouping of object parts. Parts with a different visual appearance but with the same semantic role are associated by the similarity of their occurrence distributions given the object class. In the following section, we briefly review related work. We then explain our solution in section 5.2 and demonstrate the usefulness of the approach in section 5.3. In section 5.4, we discuss our results.

5.1 Related Work

The need to model different visual entities for the same semantic entity has been discussed already, e.g., by Belongie et al. (2002) in the context of handwritten digit recognition. They state that letters like a four show more variance in appearance than, e.g., a zero, and thus should be modelled by more prototypes. Such approaches treat the different models for the same semantic entity separately, thus they have to be tested individually. They are capable of dealing with the visual variety of a single semantic entity only. Ensembles of semantically different parts are not treated, although this would be needed by part based methods for the classification of object categories. Previous work in this direction has been performed by Leibe (2004) or Epshtein and Ullman (2005). Leibe tried to associate visual parts by co-location and co-activation clustering. His approach is similar to ours as he also tries to associate parts that occur at the same location in an image, but he uses a weighted variation of the Hausdorff distance to combine visual parts. He does not apply his procedure to part frequency based object class models, as he advocates a Hough transform like voting scheme. Epshtein and Ullman (2005) use the context of parts in a probabilistic framework. They identify the geometric relation of parts co-occurring with a basic root fragment, and search for similar constellations in test images. Our approach does not need a root fragment, but creates a number of groupings based on the desired similarity of the occurrence distributions.

5.2 Semantic Recombination

The basic idea of our approach is that object parts with the same semantic meaning occur at the same location(s) on an object. For example, the mouth is always located in the lower middle of a front view of a face, no matter whether it is surrounded by a mustache or laugh lines. So in order to learn semantic groupings, we need aligned training data, i.e. object parts with the same role should occur at the same location in an image.

5.2 Semantic Recombination

$\qquad\quad\mathbf{c}_i \qquad\qquad\qquad\quad \omega \qquad\qquad\qquad p(x, y, s | \mathbf{c}_i, \omega)$

Figure 5.2: Creation of an occurrence distribution: for a given cluster and a given object class, the spatial occurrence of local features matching to the cluster gets recorded. Left: sample members belonging to the cluster (enlarged). Middle: sample image from the aligned training data. Right: the resulting distribution at a particular scale.

We start from an initial codebook containing a variety of visual structures as described in the previous chapter. We assume a general visual codebook as defined in equation (4.1).

In order to determine the semantic distance of object parts, we rely on the distribution of the occurrence of a certain structure given the object class ω. That is, for each of the clusters $\mathbf{c}_i$, an occurrence distribution

$$p^{\bullet}_{\omega,i} = p(x, y, s | \mathbf{c}_i, \omega) \qquad (5.1)$$

is built. The position of the structure is denoted by x and y, s refers to its scale. These densities can be estimated for each cluster. All local features extracted from the aligned training data are matched to the cluster centers. For each matching feature, the position and scale where it was extracted from is recorded in a histogram. The process is visualized in figure 5.2.

We define the semantic distance of two clusters to be the distance of their distribution maps

$$d^{\omega}_{\text{sem}}(\mathbf{c}_i, \mathbf{c}_j) = d(p^{\bullet}_{\omega,i}, p^{\bullet}_{\omega,j}). \qquad (5.2)$$

For d, several functions can be used. In this work, we use a distance based on normalized cross correlation as defined in equation (3.11). Since correlation is a similarity measure, not a distance measure (the value becomes bigger when the vectors are more similar), we subtract the value from the maximal possible value for normalized correlation, which is 1. We use a nonparametric representation for the occurrence distributions in the form of a three dimensional histogram (x-location, y-location and scale). Let $\mathcal{H}$ and $\mathcal{R}$ be normalized histograms with N bins, so that $\sum_{i=1}^{N} h_i = \sum_{i=1}^{N} r_i = 1$. h_i and r_i represent the individual bin values. Then, the normalized cross correlation distance is

$$d_{\text{corr}}(\mathcal{H}, \mathcal{R}) = 1 - \text{corr}(\mathcal{H}, \mathcal{R}), \qquad (5.3)$$

5 Semantic Codebooks

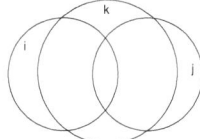

Figure 5.3: Violated transitivity condition for semantic classes.

where corr is defined in chapter 3 in equation (3.11). We can now determine whether two clusters c_i and c_j are semantically related by an indicating function $f_{\omega,\vartheta}(c_i, c_j)$, given the class ω and a threshold ϑ in the following way:

$$f_{\omega,\vartheta}(c_i, c_j) = \begin{cases} 1 & d^{\omega}_{\text{sem}}(c_i, c_j) < \vartheta \\ 0 & \text{otherwise} \end{cases} . \qquad (5.4)$$

It is important to note that we do not deal with equivalence classes here, since the transitivity condition is not met. It can easily be seen that if $f_{\omega,\vartheta}(c_i, c_k) = 1$ and $f_{\omega,\vartheta}(c_k, c_j) = 1$, it does not necessarily follow that $f_{\omega,\vartheta}(c_i, c_j) = 1$, since the similarity between their occurrence distributions does not need to be below the given threshold. This is visualized in figure 5.3. This problem is also present in natural languages: pairs of words that can be used synonymously do not have to follow transitivity conditions, e.g. the words sick↔bad as well as bad↔evil can be used interchangeably, however the words sick↔evil are not directly related any more.

In the following, we investigate the effect of grouping semantically similar parts together in a bag-of-feature classification approach. Initially, we have a part histogram $\mathcal{H}$ of local structures in dimension N, i.e. the number of clusters in the codebook.

We then have to decide which visually distinct, but semantically similar parts should be treated together. We do not directly use the semantic indicating function $f_{\omega,\vartheta}$ due to the transitivity problem mentioned above. Instead, we cluster the elements of our visual part dictionary, using the semantic similarity measure as defined in equation (5.2). In the following experiments, we use agglomerative clustering (see e.g. Jain and Dubes, 1988) with an average link paradigm, since it produces compact clusters and only relies on pairwise similarities of feature vectors. A fast clustering scheme as the MBSAS algorithm introduced in chapter 4 is not easy to apply in this case, since in the beginning of the experiments, it is not clear which hypershpere radius to choose.

The final groupings can be determined by cutting the hierarchical tree at an appropriate value. For each visual part i, we then obtain an index $s_i \in \{1, \ldots, M\}$ describing the semantic cluster membership.

We now want to combine the part frequencies of an original histogram $\mathcal{H}$ that belong to the same semantic cluster in order to obtain a more general part histogram $\mathcal{M}$ with reduced dimensionality M. The new histogram entries are given by

$$m_k = \sum_{i=1}^{N} h_i \delta(s_i, k), \ k \in \{1, \ldots, M\}, \tag{5.5}$$

where δ is the Kronecker delta function. In effect, all entries of the original histogram that are in the same semantic cluster are added together.

5.3 Experimental Evaluation

In order to show the benefits of semantic grouping of visual distinct structures, we performed various experiments for different object categories, in particular, natural as well as artificial objects. As we need aligned training data for building the location maps, we chose the categories "Faces_easy" and "Motorbikes" from the Caltech101 dataset[1] for our experiments, as they fulfill this condition very well. In the faces dataset, there are 435 images of 31 different people. Since we do not want to have images of identical people in the training and test set, we used images of the first 14 people (214 images) for training, and images from the remaining 17 people (221 images) for testing. The motorbikes dataset consists of 789 images from different motorbikes, so we used half of the images for training, the other half for testing. As negative examples for training and testing, the respective same number of images was drawn randomly from the remaining object categories.

Only gray scale information was used for feature extraction. For these experiments, we calculated GLOH features around Hessian-Laplace interest points. We used the original detector and descriptor code which can be obtained from the authors[2].

The codebook describing the visual structures under consideration was obtained by clustering 100,000 local features randomly selected from the training images. The MBSAS clustering scheme (Teynor and Burkhardt, 2007a) as explained in the previous chapter was used for this purpose, as it allows clustering a large number of features in a reasonable time. Then histograms based on the basic codebook were calculated using a sigmoid matching function.

In order to give an idea about the type of visual structures combined by our process, we show sample semantic groupings in figure 5.4. We can visually verify that combining these structures is sensible. Note the collection of different appearances for the mouth or foreheads with different hair styles.

---

[1] from http://www.robots.ox.ac.uk/~vgg/data3.html
[2] http://www.robots.ox.ac.uk/~vgg/research/affine/

5 Semantic Codebooks

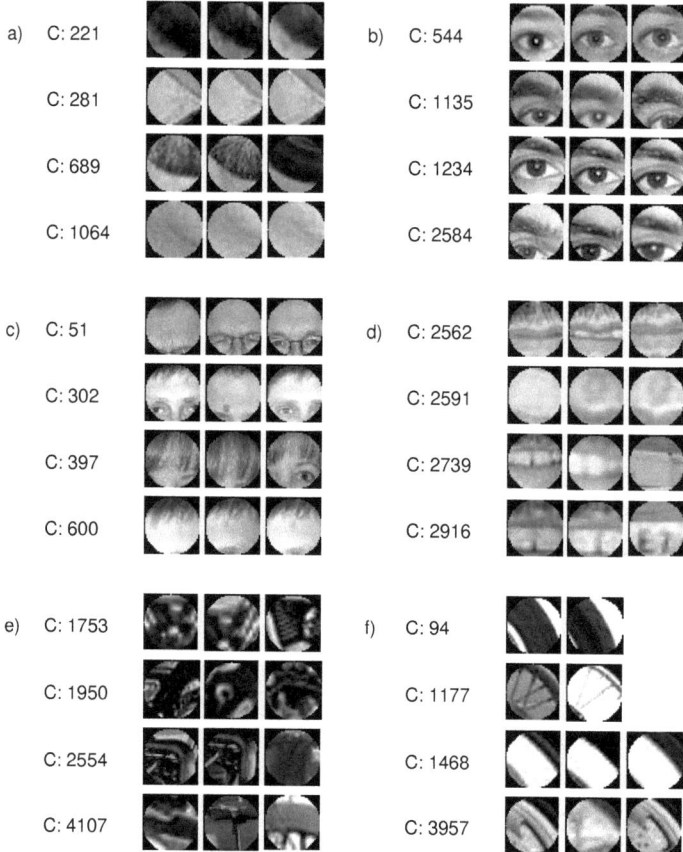

Figure 5.4: Examples of semantic groupings for the Caltech "Faces" and "Motorbikes" class as produced by the algorithm. For each semantic grouping, 4 visual clusters are shown. A visual cluster is represented by a row: the codebook number followed by at maximum 3 sample patches from the visual cluster. So the horizontal direction shows visual groupings, the vertical direction semantic groupings. We can see for the class "Faces": a) chin parts b) eyes, c) foreheads with different hair styles, d) mouth parts. For the class "Motorbikes": e) engine parts and f) wheel parts.

5.3 Experimental Evaluation

As a sample task, we deal with a two class problem where the presence of a member of a specific object class in an image should be determined. In order to show the effect of semantic clustering on different types of classifiers, we use a simple k-nearest neighbor classifier with histogram intersection as a distance measure, with $k = 3$ in our case, as well as a SVM with an histogram intersection kernel. We test the behavior for the classifiers according to different cut values in the semantic clustering step.

First, we are interested in the dimensionality of the histograms after the semantic recombination of entries. Results can be seen from the top row of figure 5.5. With increasing cut values, more and more visual clusters are combined (red curve), resulting in a lower dimensionality of the final feature vectors representing the image (green curve). At a certain point, saturation occurs. It is interesting to observe how the number of semantic groupings (i.e. the number of clusters that combine several visual structures) first rises, but then falls again (black curve). This is due to the fact that at the beginning, mainly single visual structures are combined to semantic clusters, but at higher cut values, already existing semantic clusters are combined to form bigger semantic clusters. In the extreme case, all parts related to an object would be combined in a single cluster. As we will see in the following experiments, choosing the right cut value is important. This can be done by using a validation set.

The dimensionality of the final feature vector typically does not decrease to one, as there are always visual parts that do not get combined. They either have a very distinct occurrence distribution or there were not enough training features matched to this respective cluster to create a reliable occurrence distribution. In these cases, we regarded the parts as not relevant for the class and refrained from combining them.

In the bottom of figure 5.5, we can see the results of the classification task for the different classifiers and cut values. We can see that the SVM based results are superior to the NN classifiers due to the generalization capabilities of the large margin classifier. Nevertheless we show the results for the NN classifier, since an improvement in the quality of the features can be seen more directly there. And indeed, for the NN classifier, the classification performance increases, e.g. from 91.5% for the original histogram to 95.4% for the semantically combined histogram for the motorbikes class.

The SVM cannot profit as much from the classification accuracy point of view. It even drops slightly (from 97.7% to 97.5% for the same cut values). However the number of support vectors decreases which means that we have a more "simple" decision boundary in the mapped feature space. We could save up to 14.3% of the support vectors (from 209 to 179) for the faces class with no loss in performance. Together with the reduced dimensionality of the feature vectors, this means less classification time.

For too low cut values, where many relevant parts were mapped to few histogram entries, classification performance drops for the NN classifier and the number of support vectors increases again. The specific cut values for grouping features must be determined experimentally and can be estimated using a validation set. Generally rather low cut values are already sufficient to improve performance.

5 Semantic Codebooks

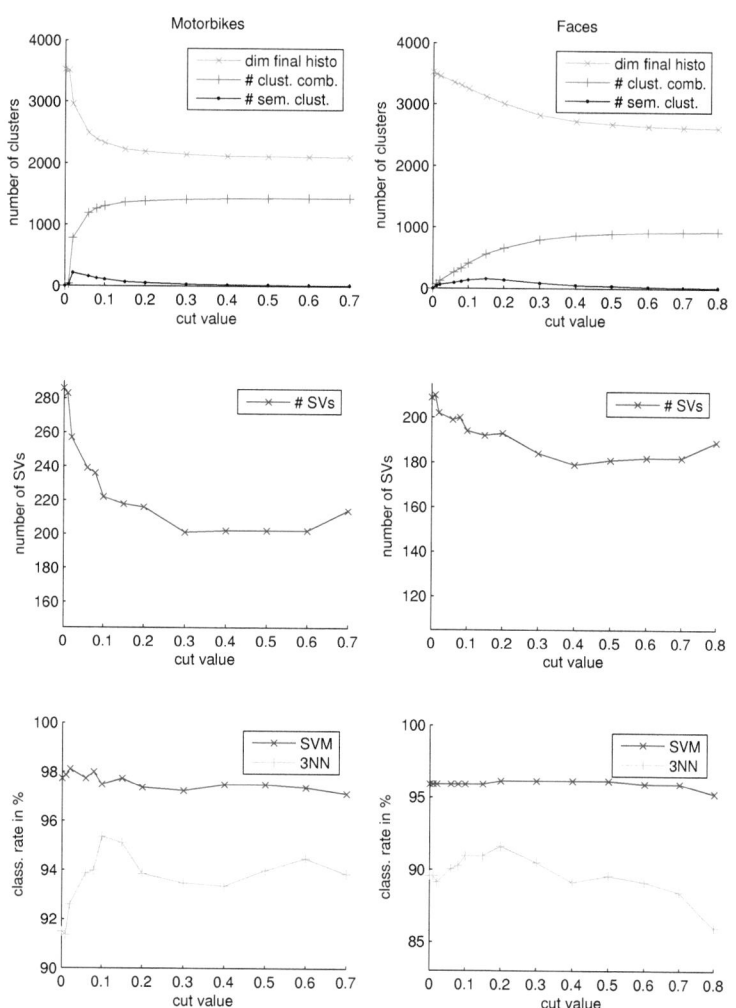

Figure 5.5: Top: Number of clusters involved in the semantic grouping. Middle: Number of support vectors used by the SVM. Bottom: classification results for the different classifiers. All numbers are listed for the different cut values in the semantic clustering step. On the left side, the results for the category "Motorbikes" are shown, on the right side the results for the class "Faces".

5.4 Discussion

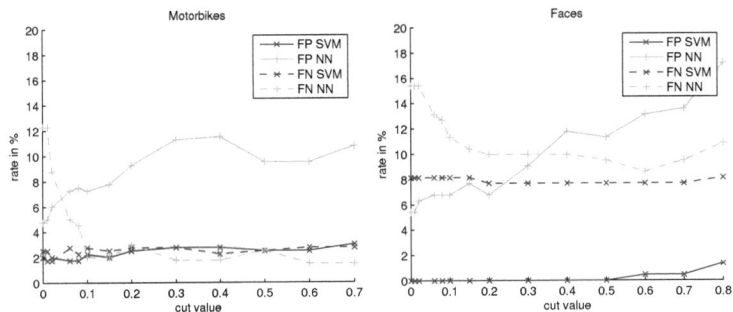

Figure 5.6: False positive rate as well as false negative rate for the different classifiers, depending on the cut value.

Looking at the misclassification types of the NN classifier depending on the threshold reveals another property of the approach: the number of false negatives (i.e. missed images containing the object) decreases, whereas the number of false positives (i.e. the number of images wrongly classified as belonging to the object class) increases. This behavior can be seen from the plots in figure 5.6. Depending on the type of application, it might be more valuable to not miss relevant images, e.g., at safety applications. As the classification results for the SVM are stable, there are not many differences for the error types there.

5.4 Discussion

Visually distinct structures may be semantically related, and cannot be grouped by their appearance only. We have shown that for object class representations based on part histograms it is beneficial to associate semantically similar parts by combining the respective visual clusters. The semantic grouping of parts can be based on the similarity of their occurrence distributions. In this way, parts that are visually distinct, but semantically similar can be associated and processed together. Having such a model has the great advantage that we do not have to train different, complex classifiers that assign the same label to an entire object. Instead, we can model the diversity in the appearance of an object at an earlier stage. Our model consists of several parts, where each part can have several visual characteristics. The decision for the identity of the object is made by a single classifier using the recombined feature vector.

Simple classifiers like a nearest neighbor classifier can directly profit from that. More complex classifiers like SVMs, that were able to deal with the diversity of semantically similar object parts in the first place, can also benefit from the process by a reduced set of support vectors and a smaller feature dimension which lead to a decrease in classification time.

The semantic mapping step can be easily incorporated into other powerful classification approaches where bag-of-feature representations are involved, like the spatial pyramid matching by Lazebnik et al. (2006), or the 3D object categorization approach by Savarese and Fei-Fei (2007). The approach is easy to implement yet effective. It can also help to reduce the number of missed objects (false negatives) in a classification task and thus increases recall.

Part II
Relating Parts

6 General Principles for Relating Parts

In this second part, we want to show how local representations that have been acquired as described in the previous chapters can be used to classify and even to localize members of visual object classes.

A variety of different models are possible to relate the local representations. Simple methods just consider the occurrence of the parts, others directly incorporate the location of the extraction. More complex methods also mind the spatial layout of the parts. The techniques can roughly be divided into the following groups, listed in increasing order of the number of parts that are set into relation:

No relationship of parts
A straightforward way is to simply consider the occurrences or frequencies of the local structures. This technique has been used for our basic experiments, and is described in more detail in chapter 7.

Pairwise relationships of parts
A more rich description of an object can be achieved by considering the pairwise relationship of its parts. This paradigm is followed, e.g., by Agarwal et al. (2004), where the co-occurrence of specific parts is indicated in a binary vector. The cluster co-occurrence histograms presented in chapter 8 also fall into this category. As shown there, they can be used as powerful features for medical image annotation (Setia et al., 2006a, 2008).

Part relations to a reference point
In this approach, object parts are related to a distinct location. This reference location does not necessarily lie on the object itself, although this is typically the case. Suitable choices are either the center of area of the object, the center of a bounding box around the object or a distinct, easy to recognize part on the object. The generalized Hough transform (Ballard, 1981) and related to that the implicit shape model by Leibe and Schiele (2003) are examples for this method. They are explained in detail in chapter 9. The use of more than one reference part leads to a so called "fan" structure, as explored in Crandall et al. (2005). These methods are related to geometric hashing (Wolfson and Rigoutsos, 1997): depending on the type of transformation to be considered two or more object points (parts) are chosen to define a coordinate system. The occurrence of all other parts is recorded relative to this reference frame. Here, no specific reference coordinate system has to be fixed, since in the learning stage, models related to all possible basis configurations are stored.

Hierarchical models

The basic scheme of hierarchical models is to first detect very simple parts that are combined to more complex parts until the final object is constructed. Work belonging to this category was performed by Bouchard and Triggs (2005), Ommer and Buhmann (2006), Epshtein and Ullman (2007) or Fidler et al. (2008).

Holistic models

In holistic models, all parts are related to another. The joint probability of all parts is evaluated. Burl (1997), Fergus et al. (2003) or Fei-Fei et al. (2004) use this paradigm. A disadvantage of this approach is that the joint densities can only be estimated for a very limited number of parts, e.g., Fergus et al. (2003) only uses 5 to 7, at maximum up to 10 parts. Another method using the entire configuration of the parts found is to look for transformation parameters that relate all object parts discovered to a model stored in the database. This model was applied, e.g., in Lowe (2004), though in the context of finding identical objects.

3D models

All methods mentioned so far typically only model objects at a certain view. As explained in chapter 1, an object might look completely distinct seen from different sides, e.g., a bicycle imaged from the front, the side or the top. Conventional approaches use multiple models for the different views of a three dimensional object. Systems explicitly modelling multiple views have recently been presented by Ponce et al. (2004) or Thomas et al. (2006). Savarese and Fei-Fei (2007) proposed a method to establish a true 3D model relating so called "canonical parts" of an object class which again consists of local representations of parts. Further ideas in this direction have been explored in Skibbe (2008), a master thesis supervised by the author.

In this work, we have explored several techniques. We present them in the following chapters and discuss their advantages and disadvantages for different types of applications.

7 Bag-of-Features Model

In this method, all spatial coherence of the parts is neglected and only the frequencies of occurring parts are considered. To emphasize the orderless nature of the approach, the figurative term *bag-of-features* or *bag-of-words* was chosen. The term *word* is used since similar techniques were originally developed in the text retrieval community. The codebook entries are thus referred to as *visual words* in this context. For object categorization the approach was first used in Csurka et al. (2004).

Each local feature $\mathbf{a}_i$ of the object is represented as a point in some D-dimensional space, where D can be rather large (e.g., $D = 128$ for SIFT features). Since we do not know anything about the distribution of the local parts in the feature space, an nonparametric density estimation procedure is applicable. Typically, histograms are chosen for this purpose. Due to the high dimensionality of the appearance feature spaces, a traditional histogram creation with a fixed partition of the individual feature dimensions as explained in chapter 3 is not applicable. In the following, we formalize the approach and show how a more general density estimate based on Parzen window density estimation can be used to obtain part histograms.

7.1 Parzen Window Density Estimation

The traditional histogram as defined in (3.15) has a number of disadvantages, e.g., it is discontinuous at the bin boundaries and a large number of bins is needed to model a distribution accurately. In our case, we have high dimensional data and an equally spaced grid for histogram creation for is impractical (as discussed in chapter 4). Instead, we are interested in the evaluation of the part density using the codebook entries $\mathbf{c}_k$, $k \in \{1, \ldots, K\}$ as bin centers. Moreover, we use equation (3.16) for histogram creation with more general windowing functions. This abstract scheme for sample density estimation using arbitrary points in space and a local weighting function was first proposed by Parzen (1962), and is thus referred to as *Parzen window* method.

The data entries can be assigned to the clusters via a nearest neighbor rule. We then get a windowing function $f'_{\mathbf{c}_k} : \mathbb{R}^D \to \{0, 1\}$ that looks like

$$f'_{\mathbf{c}_k}(\mathbf{a}) = \begin{cases} 1 & \text{if } k = \arg\min_{k'} d(\mathbf{a}, \mathbf{c}_{k'}) \\ 0 & \text{otherwise} \end{cases}, \quad (7.1)$$

7 Bag-of-Features Model

with d being a suitable distance function. The arg min procedure is assumed to solve ties in a well defined way. Using $f'_{\mathbf{c}_k}$, we obtain a Voronoi tessellation of the pattern space, given the respective cluster centers $\mathbf{c}_k$. For a probabilistically valid density estimation as defined in equation (3.16), we need to normalize the cell counts by the volume of the Voronoi cells, which cannot be calculated easily. However, this does not matter, as the partition of the space is fixed by the codebook entries and only the respective histogram entries are compared in the classification stage. In fact, by neglecting the normalization of the values by the cell volume, we obtain the integral of the assumedly constant densities inside a cell.

The individual entries of the cluster membership histogram $\mathcal{H}'(\mathbf{X}) = (h'_1, \ldots, h'_K)^\top$, for a collection of visual appearance features $\mathbf{X} = \{\mathbf{a}_1, \ldots, \mathbf{a}_M\}$, are then calculated as

$$h'_k(\mathbf{X}) = \frac{1}{M} \sum_{i=1}^{M} f'_{\mathbf{c}_k}(\mathbf{a}_i). \tag{7.2}$$

By allowing cells of variable size, we obtain an adaption to the structure of the feature space and an estimation of the distribution of the parts with a reasonable number of evaluation points.

However, when using the Voronoi tessellation, we still have the problem of discontinuities at the cell boundaries. A hard assignment of features to clusters can be too imprecise, especially if we have a rather crude partition of the high dimensional space. This can be remedied by using a continuous assignment function $f''_{\mathbf{c}_k} : \mathbb{R}^D \to [0, 1]$ which distributes the weight according to the distance to the respective cluster centers,

$$f''_{\mathbf{c}_k}(\mathbf{a}) = \frac{1}{Z_\mathbf{a}} w(d(\mathbf{a}, \mathbf{c}_k)), \tag{7.3}$$

with $w : \mathbb{R} \to \mathbb{R}$ being a suitable weighting function. Each sample point gets a weight of 1, which is then distributed between all cluster centers. I.e., $Z_\mathbf{a}$ must be set such that

$$\sum_{k=1}^{N} f''_{\mathbf{c}_k}(\mathbf{a}) = 1. \tag{7.4}$$

The weighting w function is often a Gaussian kernel, but might also have other forms, as, e.g., the sigmoid function as already presented in section 4.3.2, equation (4.3),

$$w_{\text{sig}}(x) = \frac{1}{1 + e^{\alpha(x-\varepsilon)}}. \tag{7.5}$$

7.2 Object Representation

A histogram $\mathcal{H}''(\mathbf{X}) = (h''_1, \ldots, h''_K)^\top$ with a continuous weighting function can then be calculated as

$$h''_k(\mathbf{X}) = \frac{1}{M} \sum_{i=1}^M f''_{\mathbf{c}_k}(\mathbf{a}_i). \tag{7.6}$$

Performance tests of the different histogram creation schemes have been conducted in chapter 4. We could see that the right choice of the weighting function does have an influence on recognition performance. For databases of objects with simple, distinct structures, nearest neighbor matching for histogram creation is sufficient, whereas weighted matching is superior for more diverse databases. Approaches with a fixed bin size are typically inferior.

7.2 Object Representation

Describing objects in terms of the distribution of their local parts is straightforward. The visual codebook entries $\mathbf{c}_k$ serve as seed points for the evaluation of the occurrence of structures in the feature space. An image is represented by a histogram based on local features extracted from it. The histogram entries are calculated according to equation (7.2) or (7.6), depending on the histogram construction method selected. The process is visualized in figure 7.1.

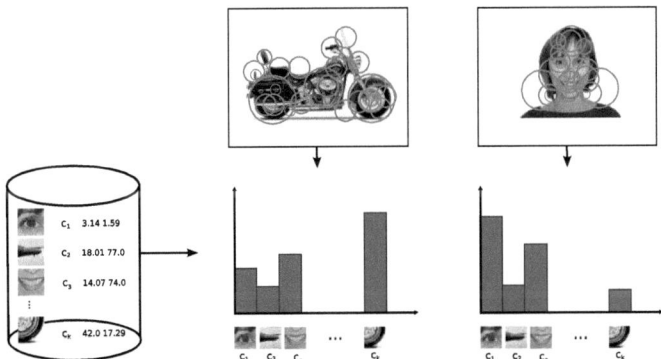

Figure 7.1: Visualization of the bag-of-features model. Left: the visual codebook. Right: features are extracted from local detections in two example image. These features are matched to the codebook entries, in order to create histograms of the occurrence of the local structures.

The histograms are then used as a feature vector for the entire object and can be used as input for established classifiers like SVMs. Since this kind of approach cannot distinguish between the object and the background, background detections are incorporated into the histogram as well. As shown in Torralba (2003), the use of contextual information can be beneficial when the object and the background are correlated, e.g., a ship is likely to be detected with water surrounding it. In certain applications, the object covers a dominant part of the image, so the histogram is mainly constructed from object parts. Many of the currently existing test databases do fulfill this constraint, e.g., the Caltech101 database. For general images though, when using histograms from the entire image, we rather perform image classification than object classification. In section 9.3.2 and 9.3.3, we show how histograms can be created only from parts that are likely to belong to a specific object.

8 Co-occurrence of Parts

The simplest way of relating parts is to look whether pairs always occur together, possibly in a specific constellation. The probability of features occurring together is expressed by co-occurrence matrices. In our case, the parts are represented by the codebook entries, thus we evaluate the co-occurrence of features belonging to the different cluster centers in the codebook. In this chapter, we propose the use of cluster co-occurrence matrices (CCM). The CCMs can be interpreted as the joint probability of two kinds of local regions to occur at a specific distance and orientation to each other. We were able to show that the use of CCMs can be very useful for classification, especially in the area of medical image annotation (Setia et al., 2006a). The CCMs can be interpreted as the joint probability of two kinds of local regions to occur at a specific distance and orientation to each other.

8.1 Related Work

The use of co-occurrence matrices was first proposed by Haralick et al. (1973) for the description of gray-level dependence in texture images. For object classification, the co-occurrence of parts was introduced by Agarwal and Roth (2002). They recorded the occurrence of parts in a specific constellation in a binary vector, so just the occurrence, not the probability for the occurrence, was captured. Amores et al. (2005) considered the constellation of parts in a probabilistic manner similar to our system, however, they do not use interest point detectors, but local features extracted from contour points obtained by a segmentation process. Our multi-dimensional co-occurrence matrix captures the statistical properties of the joint distribution of cluster indices, which describes the appearance and the structure of the image.

8.2 Cluster Co-occurrence Matrices

To create a CCM, local features extracted from interest points found in an image are matched to the entries of a visual codebook by a nearest neighbor rule. The assigned part indices as well as the location where they were extracted from are retained. We propose to build a CCM that considers the distance and the angle of co-occurring parts, resulting in a local coordinate system that is shaped like sectors of concentric circles. The coordinate system can be seen in figure 8.1.

8 Co-occurrence of Parts

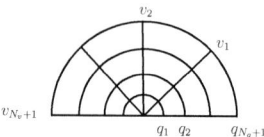

Figure 8.1: Local reference grid for determining the pairwise spatial relationship of parts.

The algorithm works as follows: we extract a set of local observations $\mathbf{F} = \{\mathbf{f}_1, \ldots, \mathbf{f}_N\}$ from an image. Each local observation $\mathbf{f} = (\mathbf{a}^\top, \mathbf{o}^\top)^\top$ consists of a vector $\mathbf{o}$ describing the location of the feature extraction, and a vector $\mathbf{a}$ describing the visual appearance of the detection. In our case here, $\mathbf{o} = (x, y)^\top$, i.e. the coordinates of an interest point. Furthermore, we have a visual codebook $\mathbf{C}$ with N_c entries. Let $\mathrm{m} : \mathbb{R}^D \to \{1, \ldots, N_c\}$ be a function returning the cluster index (label) assigned to an appearance feature $\mathbf{a}$. Typically, this will be the cluster index of the nearest cluster center in the respective feature space.

We define a vector holding the bin boundaries for the distance quantization in the co-occurrence matrix, $\mathbf{q} = (q_1, q_2, \ldots, q_{N_q+1})^\top$, where N_q is the number of quantization bins used for the radial direction and and another vector for the angle quantization, $\mathbf{v} = (v_1, v_2, \ldots, v_{N_v+1})^\top$, where and N_v is the number of quantization bins in the angular direction. The range must only cover $[0, \pi[$ since each interest point pair $(\mathbf{f}_1, \mathbf{f}_2)$ would otherwise be counted twice in the matrix. The entire process is shown illustratively in figure 8.2.

The set $\mathbf{S}^{k,\ell,i,j}$ of all interest point pairs having cluster indices k and ℓ, and that are located at a specific spatial orientation (the quantized distance and angle to each other fall into bins i and j respectively) is given as:

$$\mathbf{S}^{k,\ell,i,j} = \{ (\mathbf{f}_1, \mathbf{f}_2) \mid \mathrm{m}(\mathbf{a}_1) = k \\ \wedge \mathrm{m}(\mathbf{a}_2) = \ell \\ \wedge q_i < \|\mathbf{o}_1 - \mathbf{o}_2\|_2 < q_{i+1} \\ \wedge v_j < \angle_x(\mathbf{o}_1, \mathbf{o}_2) < v_{j+1} \}. \quad (8.1)$$

The indices are $k \in \{1, \ldots, N_c\}$, $\ell \in \{1, \ldots, N_c\}$, $i \in \{1, \ldots, N_q\}$ and $j \in \{1, \ldots, N_v\}$. The angle drawn by the vector $(\mathbf{o}_2 - \mathbf{o}_1)$ with the x-axis is measured by $\angle_x : \mathbb{R}^2 \times \mathbb{R}^2 \to [0, 2\pi[$. Now, a four-dimensional array $\mathbf{A}$ can be created, in which the cardinalities of the above sets can be stored. The array is referred to as *cluster co-occurrence matrix*, although it is not a matrix in a strict mathematical sense. The individual entries are given by:

$$\mathbf{A}_{k,\ell,i,j} = |\mathbf{S}^{k,\ell,i,j}|. \quad (8.2)$$

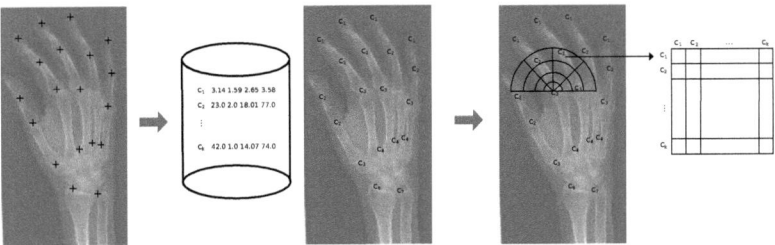

Figure 8.2: Schematic diagram depicting the creation of cluster co-occurrence features. First, local features are calculated around interest points (for better clarity, we just show a few fictive points). Then, the features are matched to the codebook, now being represented by their cluster index only. A local reference grid (a sectored semi-circle) is attached to every interest point. Pairs of co-occurring cluster indices get recorded in co-occurrence matrices, one for each sector of the semi-circle and averaged over all interest points. The radiograph image is courtesy of TM Deserno, Dept. of Medical Informatics, RWTH Aachen, Germany.

Alternatively, **A** can be seen as series of traditional two dimensional co-occurrence matrices, one for each specific sector of the coordinate system (specified by the distance i and the angle j). This is hinted in figure 8.2.

8.3 Experimental Evaluation

The features calculated in this way were applied on the IRMA 2005 database and we took part in the ImageCLEF 2006 and ImageCLEF 2007 medical image annotation benchmark, where labels had to be assigned to X-ray images.

The images used were from the IRMA project (Image Retrieval in Medical Applications), which deals with categorizing and retrieving medical images[1]. They are fully classified radiographs taken randomly from medical routine at the Aachen University Hospital, Germany. In the 2005 benchmark, the data provided consisted of 9,000 labeled training images and 1,000 test images which had to be assigned to one of 57 pre-defined categories. In 2006, there were 10,000 training and 1,000 test images, which had to be classified as one of 116 categories. The 2007 database reused these images as training and development set respectively, and a further set of 1,000 new images were used as a test set. For the 2005 and the 2006 benchmark, the evaluation was based on the error rate concerning the predefined classes, in 2007 a hierarchical classification according the IRMA-Code (Lehmann et al., 2003) was required and thus an evaluation score

---

[1] http://www.irma-project.org

that penalized misclassifications at early stages in the hierarchy was introduced. The classification for all experiments presented here was performed using a support vector machine with an histogram intersection kernel in a one-versus-rest approach. Other classification schemes were also tested, but are not subject of this work. The interest points were obtained by using the Loupias detector with a fixed scale, since all objects were pictured in the same size. The number of detections was set to 1,000. As features for the description of the individual areas the local relational features as described in section 3.3.2 were chosen, since they have been proven to be successful in texture classification. Three parameter combinations (r, r', φ, N) were used for creating the individual texture descriptors around each interest point and the respective results were concatenated. The radii for sampling the neighborhood of an interest point are denoted by r and r', φ is the angle difference and N is the number of samples taken. The individual parameter combinations chosen were $(0, 5, 0, 12)$, $(3, 6, \pi/2, 12)$ and $(2, 3, \pi, 12)$, thus the resulting feature vector consisted of $3 \times 12 = 36$ entries. The codebook contained 20 structures and was obtained by k-means clustering. The quantization factors for the distance and the angle were set experimentally to $N_q = 10$ and $N_v = 4$. The maximum distance considered was about 30% of the side length of the images. Further details on the experiments can be found in Setia et al. (2006a) and Setia et al. (2006b).

Our results were very competitive, we could obtain the best results published for the 2005 benchmark (error rate of 8.1%), the second best rank for the 2006 benchmark (error rate of 16.7%) among 27 submissions, and the 7th rank for the 2007 benchmark (error score 31.43, 3rd best performing method) among 68 submissions. The full listing of the benchmark results can be viewed in the respective publications (Setia et al., 2006a; Müller et al., 2007). In table 8.1, we list the top results achieved.

8.4 Discussion

In the evaluation of the imageCLEF benchmark, it became evident that using local information has advantages over holistic methods. The top 16 runs in the 2007 benchmark were achieved using either local image features exclusively or in combination with a global descriptor. Incorporating spatial information in the form of co-occurrences has shown to be very successful. When considering the pairwise relationship of parts, the right degree of invariance has to be chosen. Experiments with a rotation invariant descriptor (no angle quantization performed) led to inferior results for this benchmark, where all images were oriented uprightly. In other cases, rotational invariance might be necessary, e.g., for microscopy images.

A limiting factor of the co-occurrence features is the initial number of parts (clusters) that can be considered. As the size of each co-occurrence matrix depends quadratically on the number of clusters used, the number of parts cannot be too large. The richness in the description arises from setting a reduced number of possible parts into relation. Thus this kind of description is mainly suited for image categories with rather simple parts (generic corners, edges in different orientations, etc.) that become meaningful by their constellation.

8.4 Discussion

Rank	Method	Group	Result
2005 database:			**Error Rate** (%)
1.	CCMs with rel. features, 20×20×10×4 matrix, 1,000 points	Univ. Freiburg	**8.1**
2.	Sparse Histograms with position (Deselaers et al., 2006) using maximum entropy classification	RWTH Aachen	9.3
3.	Image Distortion Model (Keysers et al., 2004)	RWTH Aachen	12.6
2006 benchmark (28 submissions):			**Error Rate** (%)
1.	Sparse histograms (Deselaers et al., 2006) using maximum entropy classification	RWTH-Aachen	**16.2**
2.	CCMs with rel. features 20×20×10×4 matrix, 1,000 points	Univ. Freiburg	16.7
3.	Sparse histograms (Deselaers et al., 2006) using SVM classification	RWTH-Aachen	16.7
4.	Local and global PCA features (Florea et al., 2006)	INSA Rouen	17.2
2007 benchmark (68 submissions) :			**Score**
1.-5.	SVM-based cue integration approach (Tommasi et al., 2007)	IDIAP	**26.8–29.9**
6.	Sparse histograms (Deselaers et al., 2006), combination of four runs	RWTH-Aachen	30.9
7.	CCMs with rel. features 20×20×10×4 matrix, 1,000 points	Univ. Freiburg	31.4

Table 8.1: Top results published for the IRMA 05 database and top results achieved in the ImageCLEF 2006 and 2007 benchmark.

9 Part Relations to a Reference Point

Another way to relate the object parts is to link them via a common reference point. It is a stronger requirement than only considering pairwise relationships, but not as strict as modelling the relations of all parts to another by a joint probability model. The method is very natural and can be formulated in a straightforward way.

In section 9.1, we show how the relation of parts to a common point can be used to localize visual object class members. We review the foundations of the approach and describe the extensions we made. The result of the algorithm presented there is a probability map for the positional parameters of an object in an image. How to determine geometrically stable object parts is described in section 9.2. While the results of section 9.1 are very useful for images where we already know that the object is present, we cannot infer directly whether the object is indeed present from that. The issue of classification is thus addressed in section 9.3. There, we introduce histograms consisting of parts that agree on the spatial position of an object. We evaluate the approach on a difficult bicycle database and obtain superior results compared to global bag-of-feature approaches.

9.1 Identification of Object Parameters

In this section, we show how the precise object parameters, i.e. the location, the scale and in particular the orientation of an object, can be identified in the framework of local part representations. Taking into account the orientation of the objects is not necessary for all types of objects, since cars, e.g., are likely to be found with the wheels on the ground. For other object categories, this information is highly beneficial, since their orientation is not fixed. The additional information of the object's orientation can be useful in order to gain a deeper image understanding, e.g., whether two objects are facing each other. It can also be helpful for robot vision, e.g. to enable the robot to grasp an object better according to its orientation.

9.1.1 Related Work

An established way to determine the parameters of an entity is by means of the Hough transform. There, a probable parameter configuration θ for an object is determined by searching for maxima in a voting space. The traditional Hough transform (Duda and Hart, 1972) considers mathematical objects in form of parameterized curves (e.g. lines or circles). The generalized

9 Part Relations to a Reference Point

Hough transform (Ballard, 1981) deals with the positional parameters $\boldsymbol{\theta} = (x, y, s)^\top$ of general objects, i.e. the x-coordinate, the y-coordinate and the scale s of the object.

Hough Transform

The basic version of the Hough transform for lines as still used today was proposed by Duda and Hart (1972). They rely on the U.S. Patent 3,069,654 by P. V. C. Hough, filed already in 1962, with the name "Method and Means for Recognizing Complex Patterns".

The basic idea of the Hough transform is that all points on an analytic curve can be described by a parameterized equation. For example, a circle can be described by

$$(x - a)^2 + (y - b)^2 = r^2, \qquad (9.1)$$

where a and b are the coordinates of the center of the circle and r is the radius. For each edge point $\mathbf{x}_i = (x_i, y_i)$ observed in an image (i.e. the intensity or the gradient magnitude is above a certain threshold), there exists a number of parameter combinations that fulfill equation (9.1). This means, a variety of possible circles goes through that point. These parameter combinations are recorded in a so called accumulator array $\mathbf{A}$. $\mathbf{A}$ is a d-dimensional array with $d = \dim(\boldsymbol{\theta})$. For example, in the case of searching for circles, $d = 3$. Only a discrete parameterization can be considered, since the indices for the accumulator have to be discrete, so that the summation in equation (9.2) is computationally feasible. Thus we have to use a function $q : \mathbb{R}^{\dim(\boldsymbol{\theta})} \to \mathbb{Z}^{\dim(\boldsymbol{\theta})}$ that quantizes the parameter vector $\boldsymbol{\theta}$ to a discrete index vector $\boldsymbol{\varrho}$, i.e. $q(\boldsymbol{\theta}) = \boldsymbol{\varrho}$.

To recover the true parameters for a structure, the points observed in the image are collected in a set $\mathbf{X} = \{\mathbf{x}_1, \ldots, \mathbf{x}_N\}$. Let $\Xi_i = \{\boldsymbol{\varrho}_{i1}, \ldots, \boldsymbol{\varrho}_{iM_i}\}$ be the set of all possible quantized parameter combinations leading to the observation of point $\mathbf{x}_i$, $\boldsymbol{\varrho}_{ij} \in \mathbb{Z}^{\dim(\boldsymbol{\theta})}$. Let furthermore $s(\boldsymbol{\varrho}_{ij})$ be an array in the same size as $\mathbf{A}$, with all entries being 0, except the entry indexed by $\boldsymbol{\varrho}_{ij}$ being 1. The quantization has to be performed in such a way that all vectors $\boldsymbol{\varrho}$ reference an element inside the accumulator array, i.e. the maximum values of the individual dimensions have to be below the extents of the respective dimensions in the accumulator array $\mathbf{A}$. In $\mathbf{A}$, all parameter combinations in Ξ_i for all observed points in $\mathbf{X}$ are summed:

$$\mathbf{A} = \sum_{i=1}^{N} \sum_{j=1}^{M_i} s(\boldsymbol{\varrho}_{ij}). \qquad (9.2)$$

If a specific structure is present, the corresponding parameters are incremented more often than other possible parameter combinations. In the following, $\mathbf{A}_{\boldsymbol{\varrho}}$ is the value of the array $\mathbf{A}$ indexed by the vector $\boldsymbol{\varrho}$. The maximum in the Hough voting array should reveal an estimate $\hat{\boldsymbol{\varrho}}$ of the true, quantized object parameters

9.1 Identification of Object Parameters

$$\hat{\varrho} = \arg\max_{\varrho} \mathbf{A}_{\varrho}. \tag{9.3}$$

Using $\hat{\varrho}$, an estimate of the non-quantized object parameters $\hat{\theta}$ can be established. In order to be able to deal with noise, it is beneficial to distribute the votes in a lager parameter range according to an error model or to smooth the accumulator array (Ballard, 1981) after all votes have been collected. By using fuzzy voting techniques (Siggelkow, 2002), a greater accuracy than provided by the quantization factor can be obtained.

Generalized Hough Transform

Ballard (1981) proposed a generalized version of the Hough transform. The work introduces two extensions to the basic approach: the gradient at the image point is considered for deciding which parameter combinations are possible and a scheme is presented how non parametric curves can be modelled and detected. For this, the gradient direction at every object boundary point of an object is used as a key for entries in a so called R-table. For every gradient direction, the distance and angle to an object reference point is stored. Since for a particular gradient direction, there could be more than one parameter combination pointing to the object reference point, the R-table has a hash-table like structure. In the detection step, the R-table is used to determine possible object reference point locations.

Implicit Shape Model

Leibe and Schiele (2003) proposed a combined object categorization and figure ground segmentation framework. A central part of this framework is the Implicit Shape Model (ISM), which can be seen as a probabilistic extension of the generalized Hough transform. The ISM does not only consider isolated boundary points, but local representations of object parts as used in this thesis. The local representations vote for hypothetic object reference points. In this work, we use a similar formulation for finding probable parameter combinations for the occurrence of an object. The original formulation was not capable of identifying the orientation of objects though. When our algorithm was developed, no other part based classification system was able to detect the orientation of object class instances. In the mean time, the ISM was extended by Mikolajczyk et al. (2006) to also consider the orientation.

9.1.2 Proposed Method

In order to identify probable poses for an object, we search for parameter combinations for which the probability for the occurrence of an object of a specific class ω is high. This can be formulated by $P(\omega|\theta)$. The expression can be converted via Bayes rule into

$$P(\omega|\boldsymbol{\theta}) = \frac{p(\boldsymbol{\theta}|\omega)P(\omega)}{p(\boldsymbol{\theta})}. \tag{9.4}$$

Since we evaluate this expression for one object category at a time, and we assume that the prior probabilities for all parameter combinations $p(\boldsymbol{\theta})$ are equally likely, we solely have to evaluate $p(\boldsymbol{\theta}|\omega)$.

To determine probable parameter configurations, we rely on a set of local observations $\mathbf{F} = \{\mathbf{f}_1, \ldots, \mathbf{f}_N\}$ extracted from the image. A local observation is represented by

$$\mathbf{f} = (\mathbf{a}^\top, \mathbf{o}^\top)^\top, \tag{9.5}$$

with $\mathbf{a}$ being the visual description and $\mathbf{o} = (x, y, s, \varphi)^\top$ the positional information (x, y-coordinates) as well as the scale s and the orientation φ of the detection.

In order to identify parameter combinations with high $p(\boldsymbol{\theta}|\omega)$, we marginalize over the local observations $\mathbf{f}_i$ according to

$$p(\boldsymbol{\theta}|\omega) = \sum_{i=1}^{N} p(\boldsymbol{\theta}, \mathbf{f}_i|\omega) \tag{9.6}$$

$$= \sum_{i=1}^{N} p(\boldsymbol{\theta}|\mathbf{f}_i, \omega) p(\mathbf{f}_i|\omega). \tag{9.7}$$

The appearance $\mathbf{a}_i$ of a local part $\mathbf{f}_i$ is used to link the observations to the entries in a model database. The geometric model can be represented by a collection of individual samples, as employed in section 9.1.3. Another possibility is the use of visual codebooks and associated, part-wise object reference point distributions as used by Mikolajczyk et al. (2006). We introduce them in section 9.1.2 on page 99. The model parameters stored in the database can be used together with the positional information $\mathbf{o}_i$ of the local detection to estimate $p(\boldsymbol{\theta}|\mathbf{f}_i, \omega)$ as described in equations (9.13) – (9.17).

The probability that a certain feature belongs to the object class is reflected by $p(\mathbf{f}_i|\omega)$. If every observation is assumed to be equally significant, $p(\mathbf{f}_i|\omega)$ can be modelled by a uniform distribution.

Our method consists of two parts: the creation of a geometric model and the localization procedure itself. These are described in algorithm 9.1 and 9.2. In the following formulation, prototype parts are used directly for estimating probable object parameters. This is possible when the class to be modelled consists of few, representative parts.

9.1 Identification of Object Parameters

Algorithm 9.1: Creation of a geometric model
Input: A set of training images $\mathbf{T} = \{I_1 \ldots, I_n\}$;
Output: The geometry model $\mathbf{D}$;
Initialization: $\mathbf{D} \longleftarrow \varnothing$;
begin
    foreach $I_i \in \mathbf{T}$ **do**
        // Obtain the object reference point $\mathbf{x}^r$ and scale s^r
        $(\mathbf{x}^r, s^r) \longleftarrow$ loadObjectInfo (I_i);
        // Extract local detections from the image
        $\mathbf{F}_i \longleftarrow$ getLocalObservations (I_i);
        foreach $\mathbf{f}_{ij} = (\mathbf{a}_{ij}, \mathbf{o}_{ij}) \in \mathbf{F}_i$ **do**
            // Calculate geometry information, relative to the object reference point and scale
            $\eta_{ij} \longleftarrow$ getGeometryVector $(\mathbf{o}_{ij}, \mathbf{x}^r, s^r)$;
            // Update geometry model
            updateGeometryModel $(\mathbf{D}, \mathbf{a}_{ij}, \eta_{ij})$;
        end
    end
end

Creation of the Geometric Model

In a first stage, a set of local observations $\mathbf{F}$ is extracted from the image. The positions and scales are determined by using an interest point detector. For the recovery of the object orientation, it is also necessary to determine the orientation of the local observation. This can be done by calculating the (possibly weighted) gradient main direction of the image pixels inside the interest point area. This gradient main direction and the scale of the interest point can be used to map the image part to a standard coordinate system. The appearance features $\mathbf{a}$ are calculated in respect to this normalized area and describe the visual appearance of the local structure.

Together with the appearance information, for every local detection $\mathbf{f}_i$ in a training image, a vector

$$\eta_i = (d'_i, \varphi'_i, s'_i)^\top \tag{9.8}$$

coding the geometry gets calculated. It contains the distance of the point to the object reference point, the direction to the object reference point and the size of the object, relative to the interest point scale and orientation,

$$\mathbf{x}'_i = \mathbf{x}^r - \mathbf{x}_i \tag{9.9}$$
$$d'_i = |\mathbf{x}'_i|/s_i \tag{9.10}$$
$$\varphi'_i = \arg(x'_i + \mathrm{i}\, y'_i) - \varphi_i \tag{9.11}$$
$$s'_i = s^r/s_i \tag{9.12}$$

9 Part Relations to a Reference Point

Algorithm 9.2: Object localization

Input: Geometry model $\mathbf{D}$, query image I, number of neighbors k,
  minimum threshold to be considered ϑ
Output: estimated object parameters $\hat{\boldsymbol{\theta}} = (x, y, s, \varphi)^\top$
Initialization: 4D Voting Array $\mathbf{A} \longleftarrow 0$, *searchForSolution* $\longleftarrow$ true;
begin
  // Extract local detections from the image
  $\mathbf{F} \longleftarrow \texttt{getLocalObservations}\,(I)$;
  foreach $\mathbf{f}_i = (\mathbf{a}_i, \mathbf{o}_i) \in \mathbf{F}$ **do**
    for $j \longleftarrow 1$ *to* k **do**
      // Search for the j-th nearest neighbor in $\mathbf{D}$ regarding the appearance
      $\mathbf{n}_{ij} \longleftarrow \texttt{searchNN}\,(\mathbf{D}, \mathbf{a}_i, j)$;
      $\boldsymbol{\eta}_{ij} \longleftarrow \texttt{getGeometryInformation}\,(\mathbf{D}, \mathbf{n}_{ij})$;
      $\tilde{\boldsymbol{\theta}}_{ij} \longleftarrow \texttt{calculateHypotheticObjectParameters}\,(\boldsymbol{\eta}_{ij}, \mathbf{o}_i)$;
      $\texttt{voteForObjectParameters}\,(\mathbf{A}, q(\tilde{\boldsymbol{\theta}}_{ij}))$;
    end
  end
  while *searchForSolution* **do**
    // Find parameter set according to the maximum
    $\hat{\varrho} = \arg\max_\varrho \mathbf{A}_\varrho$;
    if $\mathbf{A}_{\hat{\varrho}} > \vartheta$ **then**
      // Check validity, e.g., perform a stability check on the votes
      valid $\longleftarrow \texttt{checkValidity}\,(\hat{\varrho}, \mathbf{X})$;
      if *valid* **then**
        searchForSolution $\longleftarrow$ false;
        $\hat{\boldsymbol{\theta}} \longleftarrow \texttt{dequantize}(\hat{\varrho})$;
      end
    else
      $\hat{\boldsymbol{\theta}} \longleftarrow -1$;
      searchForSolution $\longleftarrow$ false;
    end
    // remove the maximum
    $\mathbf{A}_{\hat{\varrho}} = 0$;
  end
end

---

with $\mathbf{x}^r = (x^r, y^r)^\top$ and s^r being the object reference point and scale. The location, scale, and orientation of the interest point $\mathbf{o}_i$ is denoted by $\mathbf{x}_i = (x_i, y_i)^\top$, s_i, φ_i, the imaginary unit by i. The superscript $'$ is attached to the normalized values. These parameters are visualized in figure 9.1. As object reference point, the center of area or the center of a bounding box can be used. In training, images containing the objects in a reference orientation ($\varphi^r = 0$) and scale are used.

9.1 Identification of Object Parameters

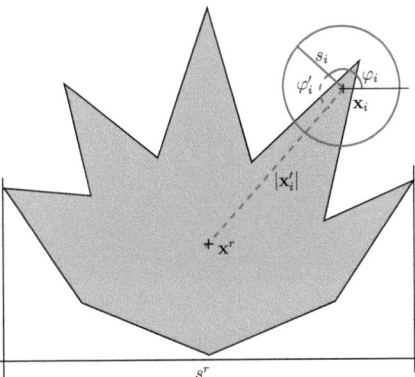

Figure 9.1: Geometry information extraction.

Object Localization

For the localization of objects in a query image, interest points and features are extracted in the same way as for the training images. We use the appearance vector of a local detection $\mathbf{f}_j$ to retrieve the k nearest neighbors (with $k = 3$ in our case) in the reference database. The geometry vector of each nearest neighbor (now referenced with η_{jn}) is used to establish a hypothesis of a possible object location, orientation and scale, relative to the positional information $\mathbf{o}_j = (x_j, y_j, s_j, \varphi_j)^\top$:

$$\tilde{d}_{jn} = d'_{jn} \cdot s_j \tag{9.13}$$
$$\tilde{x}_{jn} = \tilde{d}_{jn} \cdot \cos(\varphi_j) + x_j \tag{9.14}$$
$$\tilde{y}_{jn} = \tilde{d}_{jn} \cdot \sin(\varphi_j) + y_j \tag{9.15}$$
$$\tilde{\varphi}_{jn} = \varphi'_{jn} + \varphi_j \tag{9.16}$$
$$\tilde{s}_{jn} = s'_{jn} \cdot s_j \tag{9.17}$$

where the tilde denotes hypothetic parameters and $n \in \{1, 2, 3\}$ the index of the current nearest neighbor.

All parameter sets $\tilde{\boldsymbol{\theta}} = (\tilde{x}_{jn}, \tilde{y}_{jn}, \tilde{\varphi}_{jn}, \tilde{s}_{jn})^\top$ are quantized and vote for an entry in a four-dimensional accumulator array. We employ a fuzzy voting approach disseminating the vote not only to the exact bin, but also to the neighbors to cope with small object deformations. Matched parts with a distance above a threshold get discarded. In order to obtain the object parameters, we search for maxima in the Hough space. The voting process is visualized in figure 9.2. In the first

9 Part Relations to a Reference Point

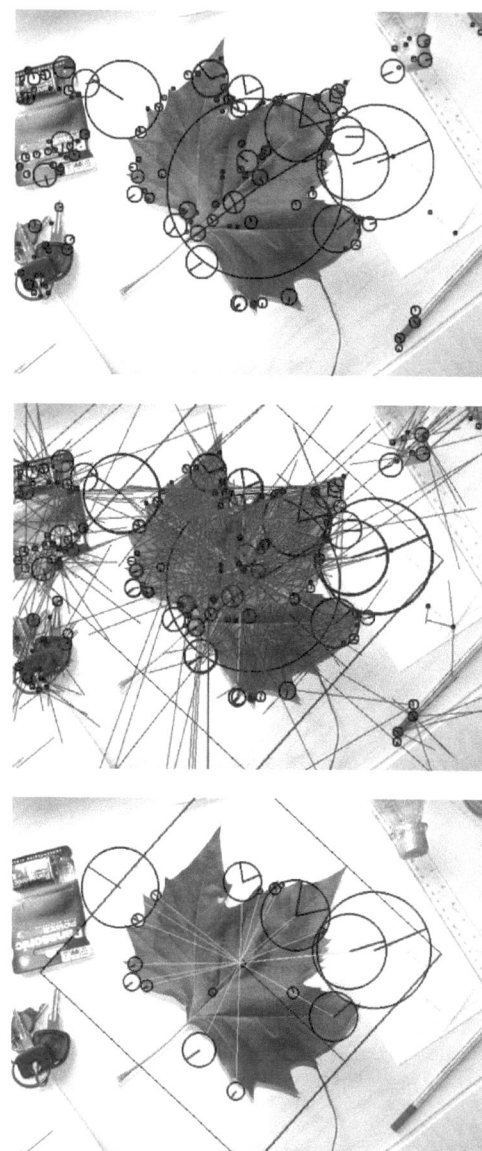

Figure 9.2: Localization process.

image, all interest points with their scale and orientation are shown. The appearance features extracted at these points are used for a k-nearest neighbor search. In the second image, the resulting votes for possible object centers are displayed (all scales and rotations simultaneously). The hypothetic center points are connected with the respective interest points that voted for them by a red line. The last image shows the location and orientation of the most probable object bounding box as indicated by the maximum of the voting array, together with the interest points supporting this hypothesis.

Object Reference Point Distributions

In the above formulation, the geometric model was represented by a collection of individual samples. This is feasible for simple object categories with a limited number of structures. For more complex objects and general databases, a more compact representation is required. We thus make use of the part dictionaries. For each codebook entry c_j in a codebook C, probable locations of an object reference point can be described by an object reference point distribution

$$p_{\omega,j}^\circ = p(\eta | c_j, \omega) \qquad (9.18)$$

for a given class ω, $\eta = (d', \varphi', s')^\top$. This parameter vector references an object of scale s', located at a distance d' and angle φ' from an object part belonging to cluster c_j. All entities are normalized by the scale and possibly by the orientation of the part. The connection between a local detection f_i and the $p_{\omega,j}^\circ$ is established by matching the appearance a_i to the entries in the codebook C. The $p_{\omega,j}^\circ$ associated to a matched codebook entry c_j can be used for estimating probable object parameters $\hat{\theta}$.

The object reference point distributions $p_{\omega,j}^\circ$ are closely related to the location distributions $p_{\omega,j}^\bullet$ as defined in equation (5.1) in chapter 5 for the semantic grouping of parts. The $p_{\omega,j}^\circ$ describe the occurrence of the object (represented by the reference point as well as the orientation and scale) relative to the local part, whereas $p_{\omega,j}^\bullet$ describe the occurrence of a part relative to the object. The two distributions can be transformed into each other. In the original formulation of $p_{\omega,j}^\bullet$, the rotation of the object is not considered, but could be incorporated easily.

The distributions $p_{\omega,j}^\circ$ are learned by matching the visual appearance a_i of the local detections obtained from aligned training data to the codebook entries c_j of a general codebook. The function updateGeometryModel in algorithm 9.1 is changed so that the location parameters η_{ij} of the object reference point are recorded for each cluster separately. When all samples are collected, normalized histograms are created from the detections.

The parameter estimation step in algorithm 9.2 is altered accordingly: the appearance vector a_i of the local observation is matched to the codebook. The respective $p_{\omega,j}^\circ$ can be used together with the positional information o_i to obtain a distribution for probable object parameters. This

9 Part Relations to a Reference Point

distribution can be used directly for voting in the accumulator array, thus the voting maps obtained in this way are typically more dense. This is especially true if only a small number of local observations can be made in the search image. A sample voting map using object reference point distributions for the class bicycles can be seen from figure 9.8 in section 9.3 in the context of object classification.

9.1.3 Experimental Results

In this section we test the capability of our algorithm to recover the position, the scale as well as the rotation of objects. For our experiments, we decided to use leaves as an object class since they are likely to be found in any rotational position in an image and are naturally to be found in many variations. For the first experiments, we use the Caltech leaf database[1]. There are 6 different leaves from 3 tree types, each leaf photographed 10 times in a cluttered office background, resulting in a database of 180 images.

In order to determine the local appearance of an object, we extract Difference of Gaussian (DoG) interest points in the images and compute SIFT features at these locations. We use the program provided by D. Lowe[2] for this task. For each key-point, we obtain a location as well as a size and an orientation information from the detector. The orientation is the dominant gradient direction of the patch. We relax the discriminativity of the 128 dimensional SIFT descriptors while still coding the main characteristics of the patch: we perform a PCA on the feature vectors and only use a reduced set of coefficients. Using two thirds of the dimensions turned out to be sufficient in our experiments (see discussion on page 102 and results in figure 9.3).

We rotated the test images randomly and recorded the angles. Since the DoG interest points found along edges are removed by the SIFT detector, the newly introduced edges in the resulting images do not affect the localization procedure. In order to also have a database with images of naturally rotated leaves for our experiments, we created a database by ourselves, where the leaves were photographed in fixed orientations in front of office backgrounds similar to the Caltech database. We photographed 10 different leaves of a tree in 8 orientations and in 7 different scenes, resulting in 560 images. The images are of size 640×480. Only gray scale information was used.

Training was performed using images with the objects in a reference orientation and size. The training leaves were segmented in order to calculate the center of area as the object reference point and to avoid background patches in the reference database. Only local detections whose area intersected the segmented object were used. We performed cross-validation tests in a leave-one-object-out approach, i.e. the same leaf instance was never used for training and testing, despite being photographed in front of different backgrounds.

---

[1] http://www.robots.ox.ac.uk/~vgg/data3.html
[2] http://www.cs.ubc.ca/spider/lowe/keypoints/siftDemoV4.zip

9.1 Identification of Object Parameters

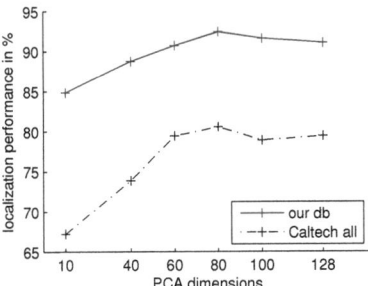

Figure 9.3: Localization performance in respect to the feature dimension (after PCA transformation).

For all experiments, the Hough space was quantized to 30 bins for the x direction, the y direction and the angle, as well as 10 bins for the scale. For the Caltech leaf database, the experiments were performed on the 3 leaf classes separately as well as on the entire dataset. This shows that the approach is capable of localizing objects despite having more than one object class in the reference database. In the following experiments, the geometry model is represented by individual samples.

We tested the best descriptor dimensionality, the accuracy of the estimated object reference point, the orientation of the object as well as the altogether localization accuracy (position and orientation). Scale changes were not tested explicitly, since all leaves in the Caltech database were about the same size, and our own database was created in a similar way.

Eliminating Unstable Votes

Sometimes many votes for a specific parameter combination come from a single direction. These points are very unstable and might result from clutter in the scene. The problem is visualized in figure 9.4. We favor parameter sets that get votes from different directions. To verify this, we also record the directions the votes came from. We quantize the angles into n sectors and require the votes to come from at least two non neighboring sectors, ensuring a minimum angle between voting interest points of at least $2\pi/n$. In our case, we use 8 sectors resulting in a required angle of minimum $45°$.

9 Part Relations to a Reference Point

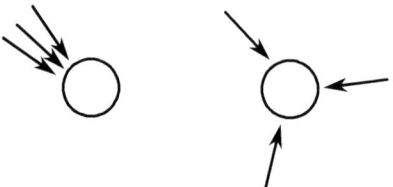

Figure 9.4: Left: unstable configuration with three votes coming from a single direction, right: stable configuration with three votes from different directions.

Descriptor Dimensionality

In our experiments, we use a PCA transformed version of the SIFT descriptor as features. The SIFT features were initially developed for the detection of identical object instances in images, and are therefore very discriminative. Since we deal with visual object classes, we only use a portion of the PCA features to capture the general appearance of a patch, but not the minor details. We performed tests to determine the optimal number of coefficients for our database by measuring the total localization accuracy (position and orientation) of the algorithm for different numbers of PCA coefficients. The tests were performed on our own database as well as on the entire Caltech leaf dataset. As can be seen in figure 9.3, the performance is poor for a small number of coefficients, steadily increasing until two thirds of the coefficients are used. Using higher numbers decreased the performance slightly again. The reason for this might be that the original SIFT descriptor was designed to be very discriminative, in order to find parts of identical objects. Reducing the discriminativity a bit by just using a fraction of the PCA coefficients of the transformed descriptor is thus beneficial. Of course, using too little coefficients also spoils the performance. About 80 dimensions turned out to be best in our experiments, so we used this number in all of the following tests.

Results for Object Position

A good estimate of the object reference point is important for a precise object localization, so we first verified this. We list the performance of the position estimates with tolerance 1 and 1.5 times the bin width of the localization grid. When within the respective bound, the position estimate is considered correct, otherwise false.

The results in table 9.1 show that for the Caltech tree 2 category and our own leaves the position estimates are very good, with inferior results for the Caltech tree 1 and tree 3 categories. Inspecting the wrong estimates for the tree 1 category revealed a reason for this. The algorithm produces competing hypotheses for objects with partial rotation symmetric structures. A subset

9.1 Identification of Object Parameters

	class. rate for tolerance		avg. distance (pixel)
	$\Delta = 1$ bin	$\Delta = 1.5$	
Caltech all	86.1	94.4	24.8
Caltech tree 1	81.7	91.7	27.2
Caltech tree 2	95.0	96.7	24.7
Caltech tree 3	88.3	95.0	34.5
own db	96.1	98.9	11.7

Table 9.1: Objects detected in the correct position in % and average distance of the estimated to the true reference point in pixel.

of the leaf "fingers" might hint at a different position (and orientation) of the leaf. For this specific dataset, mainly one leaf instance (with two main leaflets instead of one) was responsible for the errors. The algorithm chooses one of the two leaflets as the main leaflet and estimates the position accordingly.

Such errors are easy to remedy, since we know the rough position and orientation of the object. We can, e.g., correlate an object mask in a small neighborhood of the estimated object position to refine the parameters. To verify that we only need to test a small vicinity, we increase the tolerance to 1.5 times the bin width. We can see that the performance is strongly increased. In table 9.1, we list the average distance in pixels of the estimated to the real object reference point. For correct matches, the distance is usually smaller. This average value is heavily biased by false detections (estimated reference points not related to the object), that are usually far away from the real object reference point.

Results for Object Orientation

We are not only capable of detecting the position of object class instances in an image, the main novelty in our approach is that we are also able to detect the orientation. Since we deal with natural objects, we allow a tolerance of $\pi/12$ in either direction for the detected rotation angle from the true value. For bigger differences, the estimated angle is considered false. The results for this experiment can be seen in table 9.2.

The results are quite well, only the orientation assignment for the Caltech tree 1 category is less precise. Again, the wrong estimates are mainly images from the outlier leaf instance with the two leaflets. Since for this leaf, no other images with this geometry can be found in the database, we consider this a plausible error. Please note that despite the less accurate position estimate for the Caltech leaves of type 3, the orientation was estimated correctly in most cases.

9 Part Relations to a Reference Point

	class. rate for $\Delta = \pi/12$
Caltech all	86.7
Caltech tree1	73.3
Caltech tree2	93.3
Caltech tree3	91.7
own db	94.3

Table 9.2: Objects detected in the correct orientation in %.

	class. rate for tolerance	
	$\Delta = 1$ bin	$\Delta = 1.5$ bins
Caltech all	80.6	86.7
Caltech tree1	68.3	73.3
Caltech tree2	93.3	93.3
Caltech tree3	85.0	91.7
own db	92.3	94.3

Table 9.3: Objects detected in the correct position and orientation in %.

Results for Object Position together with Orientation

In the last test we show the total localization performance (position and orientation) of the approach, with the results listed in table 9.3. Images, where either the reference point distance or the orientation was not within the tolerance were considered false. Again, we list the results for distance threshold of 1 as well as 1.5 times the bin distance. Example results for our database can be seen in figure 9.5.

The results show that for geometrically stable objects, a very good overall performance can be achieved. Incorrect estimates are mainly due to a slightly inaccurate position hypothesis; orientation estimates were correct in most cases. This is especially visible when comparing the overall performance for the wider threshold with the orientation only evaluation: it is mostly the same for both experiments. As described above, the rough position hypotheses can be refined using the first position estimate as a seed.

When looking at the results for the tests involving all Caltech leaf categories, we verify that the approach is capable of localizing different leaf instances with multiple leaf types in the reference database. The result for the whole database is about the same compared to the average of the individual categories.

9.1 Identification of Object Parameters

Figure 9.5: Example results for object localization on our database.

9.1.4 Discussion

We presented a method to determine the precise location parameters of visual object class members using local patch information. We could verify the capability to estimate the correct position as well as the angle for natural objects in cluttered scenes. Especially the orientation estimation works very well.

A prerequisite for the approach is that enough stable interest points can be found on an object. Here other scale invariant interest point detectors could be used, to further improve the results.

The voting procedure as described in this section is intended to recover the positional parameters of an object. Classification is done implicitly by the fact that the local appearance of the different leaf types in the Caltech database are distinct. The local parts of the query object are matched more likely to parts of their own class, so the object reference point distributions can be stored for different kinds of leaf types simultaneously.

9.2 Geometrically Stable Object Parts

For every object class, there will be parts that are geometrically more stable than others, i.e. they can tell us more about the position of the object than other parts. As a simple example, identifying the wheels of a car tells us more about its position than a simple bar. We can use these stable object parts to obtain pronounced maxima in the Hough space for object parameter estimation. In the following, we will detail how geometrically stable object parts can be found.

A measure for the uncertainty associated with a random variable is the *Shannon Entropy* or the *Information Entropy*. The Shannon Entropy of a discrete random variable X, that can take on possible values $\{\mathbf{x}_1, \ldots, \mathbf{x}_N\}$ is defined as

$$H(X) = E[\mathfrak{J}(X)], \qquad (9.19)$$

i.e. the expected value E of the information content $\mathfrak{J}$ of X. The information content of a random variable X is associated with the probability of the occurrence of this event and thus modelled as

$$\begin{aligned}\mathfrak{J}(X) &= \log\left(\frac{1}{p(X)}\right) & (9.20) \\ &= -\log(p(X)). & (9.21)\end{aligned}$$

It is typically measured in "bits", i.e. the logarithm to the base of two is taken. Substituting (9.21) into (9.19) we get

$$\begin{aligned}H(X) &= E[\mathfrak{J}(X)] & (9.22) \\ &= \sum_{i=1}^{N} p(\mathbf{x}_i) \log\left(\frac{1}{p(\mathbf{x}_i)}\right) & (9.23) \\ &= -\sum_{i=1}^{N} p(\mathbf{x}_i) \log(p(\mathbf{x}_i)). & (9.24)\end{aligned}$$

The possible values vary between 0 (i.e. one outcome is certain) and $\log(N)$ (i.e. all outcomes are equally probable), where N is the number of possible values for the discrete random variable. We thus normalize the entropy by the number of outcomes in this way, obtaining the normalized entropy:

$$H'(X) = \frac{1}{\log N} H(X). \qquad (9.25)$$

9 Part Relations to a Reference Point

Now in order to determine parts that are geometrically stable with respect to the object reference point of a given class ω, we calculate the Shannon Entropy on the histogram representation of their object reference point distributions $p^{\circ}_{\omega,j}$. Using the histograms, the object reference point distributions are already discretized and the Shannon Entropy can be applied directly. Now the parts can be sorted according to their Shannon entropy and stable as well as unstable parts can be identified.

In the following, we describe initial tests to visually verify the proposed method. We used the same images, features and codebooks as for the experiments in section 5.3, i.e. Caltech101 images from the classes "Faces_easy" and "Motorbikes", GLOH features extracted from Hessian-Laplace interest points and an MBSAS codebook with 3,528 visual words. The $p^{\circ}_{\omega,j}$ were computed by matching the local detections of the training images to the codebook entries using a three nearest neighbor scheme and recording their normalized object parameters in a respective histograms. The object reference point was assumed to be in the middle of the training images and the object to be pictured at the same scale in all images (relative to the image boundary). The quantization factors for the parameter space were $5 \times 12 \times 3$, with the first dimension being the normalized distance to the object reference point, the second dimension the angle to the object reference point and the third dimension the scale of the object. We neglect the orientation since all objects are aligned. Each cluster had to be matched by detections stemming from more than 10% of the images in order to be valid, and the maximum distance of an interest point to the object center was allowed to be 10 times the interest point scale. Other matches too far away from the object center (relative to its own size) are very unstable. These restrictions resulted in 370 valid object reference point distributions for the class faces, and in 1021 valid distributions for the class motorbikes. For each $p^{\circ}_{\omega,j}$, the normalized Shannon entropy was calculated and the parts sorted accordingly.

Sample parts that are geometrically stable (i.e. they have a small Shannon entropy) can be seen from figures 9.6 and 9.7. In order to characterize the appearance of the respective part, some visual representations of the part (i.e. members of the respective cluster) are shown together with the $p^{\circ}_{\omega,j}$. Each scale dimension is shown as an individual layer, with each layer representing the location of the object center point in polar coordinates. The scale of the object is coded as multiples of the interest point scale. In order to better visualize the distributions, they are additionally presented as a back-projection to a sample training image representing the class to show where the parts came from. It is then equivalent to an occurrence distribution $p^{\bullet}_{\omega,j}$ as defined in section 5.2, equation (5.1), using polar coordinates. Transparent regions mean that no parts originated from the respective region, the color codes the probability of the occurrence.

Preliminary experiments have shown that using only stable parts to recover probable occurrence parameters for an object lead to more pronounced maxima in voting space. In a classification setting however, where all maxima are checked whether an object is indeed present, the restriction to only very stable parts has shown no clear advantage. The visual inspection of the most stable clusters is still useful to check the the plausibility of the features. Furthermore, the most stable clusters can be used to serve as reference parts for the object class. In the experiments in the next chapter, we discarded the geometrically most unstable parts to obtain the best results.

9.2 Geometrically Stable Object Parts

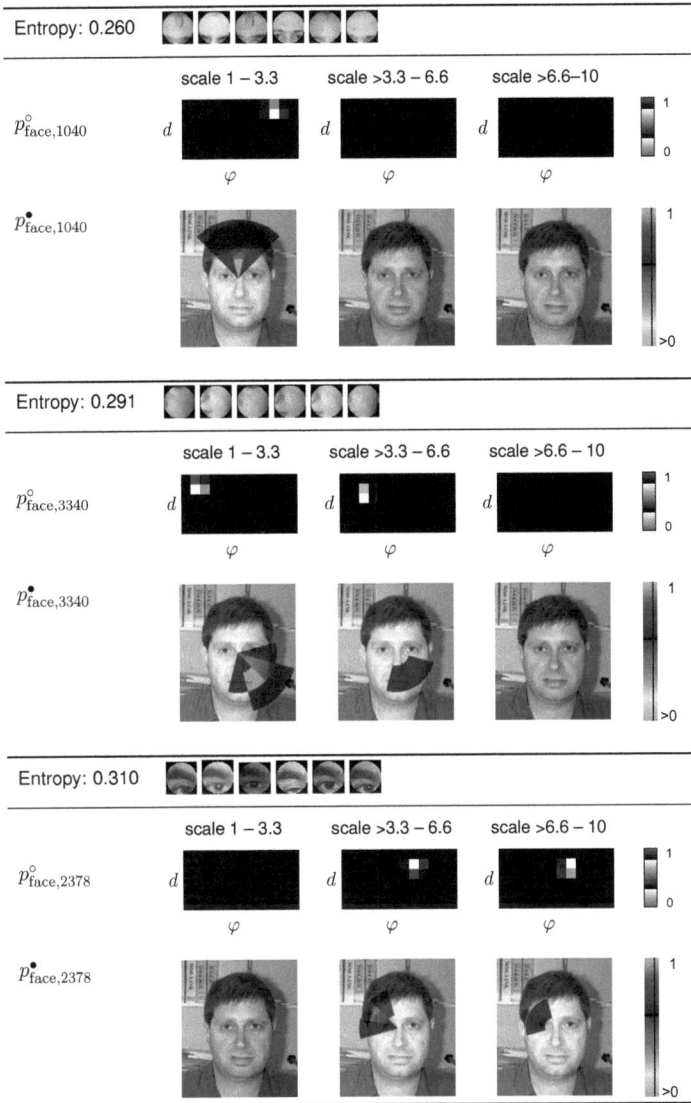

Figure 9.6: Three examples for geometrically stable parts for the class faces. For each cluster, the Shannon entropy is listed together with some sample patches in the top row. Below, the object reference point distribution and the corresponding part occurrence distribution is visualized.

9 Part Relations to a Reference Point

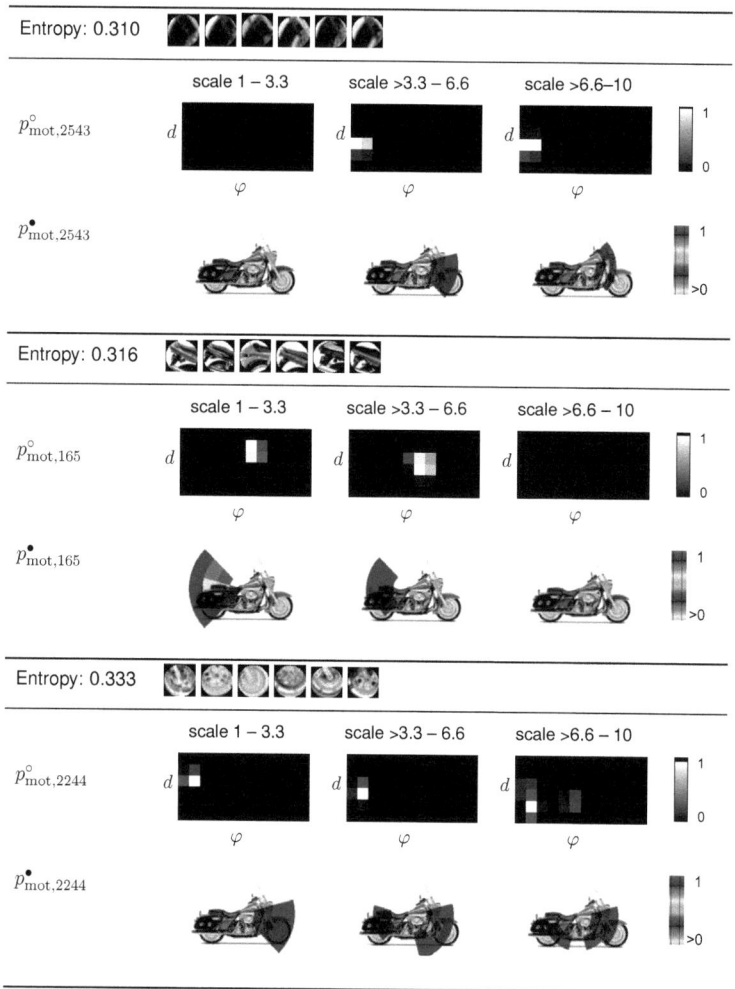

Figure 9.7: Three examples for geometrically stable parts for the class motorbikes. For each cluster, the Shannon entropy is listed together with some sample patches in the top row. Below, the object reference point distribution and the corresponding part occurrence distribution is visualized.

9.3 Object Classification

A voting based approach as presented in the previous section has the advantage that a probable position of the object can be identified easily. But transferring the probability for a particular parameter configuration to a decision function whether an object is present in the image or not is not applicable. Although the strength in which the most probable parameter combination is found can give us some evidence for the presence of an object. It is not reliable, since the calculation of the probabilities was done already assuming the object is present. In figure 9.8, we show the probability maps for possible location and scale parameters for objects of the class bicycles. In one image, indeed a bicycle is present, in the other, the maxima stem from random detections. These random detections can also accumulate in images containing a bicycle, resulting in additional maxima.

In previous experiments we have seen that histograms of local parts are an effective way for representing the content of an image. Whenever an object is dominant in an image, or the background is related to the object, histograms are a suitable descriptor for visual object class members. However, as soon as the background clutter is not related to the object or becomes dominant because the object is relatively small, histograms of the entire image are not suitable any more. A naive way to solve this problem is to use sliding windows in different sizes and

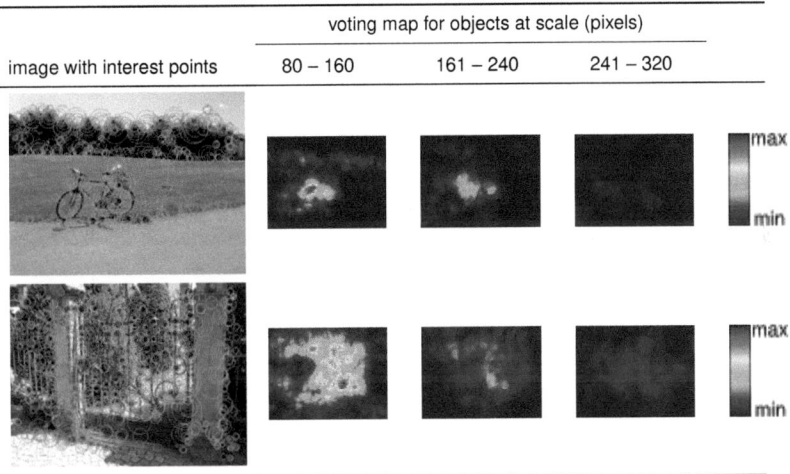

image with interest points	voting map for objects at scale (pixels)		
	80 – 160	161 – 240	241 – 320

Figure 9.8: Voting space for probable location and scale parameters given the class bicycles. Dark red regions indicate the most probable parameter combinations, dark blue regions refer to unlikely parameter values, given the image and the object class.

9 Part Relations to a Reference Point

orientations (see e.g. Laptev, 2006), and to compute the histograms only inside these regions. A direct evaluation of all possible subwindows is very costly. Typically, the sliding windows are rectangular to enable the use of fast techniques for local histogram calculation (e.g. Lampert et al., 2008). Using rectangular windows has a drawback though: as the objects can have an arbitrary form, background features might still be incorporated into the histogram even if the rectangular bounding box is of the right size. Scanning the image with an object mask prevents the use of fast techniques and thus is expensive.

In this work, we propose to merge the part based object parameter estimation with the creation of local part histograms for object classification. We have explored two variants: in a first approach, a regional histogram is created from a local region induced by a probable object parameter combination θ. This will be formulated in 9.3.2. Another, more sophisticated method is presented in section 9.3.3: there, we propose to construct histograms only from parts that agree on a specific parameter combination θ, i.e. parts that are spatially coherent.

To decide whether an object of a specific class is present in an image or not, the parameter combination θ is searched, for which $p(\theta|\omega)$ is maximized, and then regional or SCP histograms are calculated using this θ. These histograms can be used as input for any feature based classifier, e.g., SVMs. To not be sensitive against accidental accumulations of random votes, and in order to enable multiple detections, not only the parameter combination with the highest probability should be utilized, but all parameter combinations above a certain confidence value. An experimental evaluation of the techniques presented in the following can be found in 9.3.4.

9.3.1 Related Work

As described in section 9.1.1, Leibe et al. (2008) and Mikolajczyk et al. (2006) also use a Hough transform like voting scheme to recover probable object parameters in their recognition systems. The actual classification mechanisms are fundamentally different though. In Leibe et al. (2008), the recognition stage relies on a figure ground segmentation of the object in question, based on the local detections. Points inside the hypothetic object boundary get sampled densely to refine the object boundary initially found. The process requires pixel wise segmentation masks for the training objects. The final decision on whether and where an object is present in an image is made using a minimum description length (MDL) hypothesis verification stage. In Mikolajczyk et al. (2006), the classification is done by evaluating the likelihood ratio between the probabilities that the object with a specific parameter combination is present or absent.

9.3.2 Regional Part Histograms

In the following, we define a histogram $\mathcal{H}^{R_\theta}$ constructed only from parts that lie inside a region derived from a specific object parameter combination θ. This region can be an object mask in the shape of the object. In a more simple case, a rectangular bounding box can be employed. The regional part histogram is defined as

9.3 Object Classification

$$\mathcal{H}^{R_\theta}(\mathbf{F}) = (h_1^{R_\theta}, \ldots, h_K^{R_\theta}). \qquad (9.26)$$

for a set of local observations $\mathbf{F} = \{\mathbf{f}_1, \ldots, \mathbf{f}_M\}$ and an object parameter vector θ. K is the number of parts, D is the dimension of the appearance features and M is the number of local observations. Let $f_{\mathbf{C}_k}^{R_\theta} : \mathbb{R}^D \to \{0,1\}$ be a function, that indicates whether an interest point matches to a specific cluster and additionally lies inside a region derived from θ.

$$f_{\mathbf{C}_k}^{R_\theta}(\mathbf{f}) = \begin{cases} 1 & \text{if } f'_{\mathbf{C}_k}(\mathbf{a}) \wedge f^{\mathrm{r}}(\mathbf{o}, \theta) \\ 0 & \text{otherwise} \end{cases}. \qquad (9.27)$$

$f'_{\mathbf{C}_k} : \mathbb{R}^D \to \{0,1\}$ tells whether the feature's local appearance matched to a respective cluster (as defined in (7.1)), and $f^{\mathrm{r}} : \mathbb{R}^{\dim(\theta)} \times \mathbb{R}^{\dim(\theta)} \to \{0,1\}$ decides whether the interest point with location parameters o lies inside the region induced by θ. For simplification of the notation, the dependence of the equations on the class ω is neglected.

The individual histogram entries $h_k^{R_\theta}$ are then given by

$$h_k^{R_\theta} = \frac{1}{Z} \sum_{i=1}^{M} f_{\mathbf{C}_k}^{R_\theta}(\mathbf{f}_i), \qquad (9.28)$$

where Z is a normalization constant that assures that $\sum_k h_k^{R_\theta} = 1$.

9.3.3 Histograms of Spatially Coherent Parts

Besides considering all parts inside a region, a histogram can be constructed only from parts that agree on a specific parameter combination θ. This is more strict than considering all parts inside an entire region. It can be beneficial in cases where the object is occluded, since applying a bounding box or an object mask would incorporate regions that do not belong to the object. In the following, we define *Histogram of Spatially Coherent Parts (SCP)* as

$$\mathcal{H}^{\mathrm{SCP}_\theta}(\mathbf{F}) = (h_1^{\mathrm{SCP}_\theta}, \ldots, h_K^{\mathrm{SCP}_\theta}) \qquad (9.29)$$

for a set of local observations $\mathbf{F} = \{\mathbf{f}_1, \ldots, \mathbf{f}_M\}$ and a parameter vector θ. Let $f_{\mathbf{C}_k}^{\mathrm{SCP}_\theta} : \mathbb{R}^D \to [0, 1]$ be a membership function that indicates how strongly a feature vector voted for a specific cluster and a given parameter combination,

$$f_{\mathbf{C}_k}^{\mathrm{SCP}_\theta}(\mathbf{f}) = \begin{cases} p(\eta|\mathbf{c}_k, \omega) & \text{if } f'_{\mathbf{C}_k}(\mathbf{a}) \wedge q(f^{\mathrm{P}}(\mathbf{o}, \eta)) = q(\theta) \\ 0 & \text{otherwise} \end{cases}. \qquad (9.30)$$

$f^{\mathrm{p}} : \mathbb{R}^{\dim(\theta)} \times \mathbb{R}^{\dim(\theta)} \to \mathbb{R}^4$ calculates the object parameters for a given geometry vector η relative to position of the local detection $\mathbf{o}$. $q : \mathbb{R}^{\dim(\theta)} \to \mathbb{Z}^{\dim(\theta)}$ is a quantization function, that returns a discrete index vector. Also here, the dependence of the equation on class ω and the precise quantization function is neglected.

The individual histogram entries $h_k^{\mathrm{SCP}\theta}$ are then given by

$$h_k^{\mathrm{SCP}\theta} = \frac{1}{Z'} \sum_{i=1}^{M} f_{\mathbf{c}_k}^{\mathrm{SCP}\theta}(\mathbf{f}_i), \qquad (9.31)$$

Z' is a normalization constant that assures that $\sum_k h_k^{\mathrm{SCP}\theta} = 1$.

9.3.4 Experimental Evaluation

In this section we evaluate the classification performance of a Support Vector Machine using our novel approach, i.e. using regional as well as SCP histograms. We also test a combination of these features, in order to see whether the two types of histograms complement one another.

Dataset

We have collected a difficult dataset of 500 images in an urban environment. The images are of size 480×360. In half of the images, side views of bicycles are present, in the other half, they are absent, but the scenes are very similar to the ones containing bicycles. The bicycles contained in the test set cover only a small fraction of the image area and are sometimes partially occluded. The test images were selected in such a way that we cannot infer the content of the image easily by its background. This can be seen by the fact that a global part histogram performs poorly on this dataset. We wanted to assess whether we can elaborate on this. The training set contains bicycles in a more tidy environment to facilitate the learning process. For these training images, manual bounding boxes around the bicycles were created. We used 200 images for training, and 300 images for testing. In each case, one half of the images contained bicycles, the other half not.

We compiled this dataset, since no other database that is publicly available met our requirements. These databases either demand a pure localization task (e.g. UIUC cars, TU-Darmstadt motorbikes), the background of the images is highly correlated (e.g. Caltech motorbikes, faces) or the objects are photographed in arbitrary poses (e.g., the PASCAL challenge). We wanted to avoid a pure localization task, since we have already shown in section 9.1.3 that the approach is capable of doing so.

Feature calculation

We extracted Hessian-Laplace interest points from the images and calculated rotation sensitive GLOH features at these locations. 50,000 random detections from the training set were used as input to the MBSAS clustering algorithm. We obtained 2,756 clusters centers, i.e. different visual parts.

The object reference point distributions were learned by using the bounding box data of the training images. The object reference point was chosen to be the center of the bounding box. With this, normalized geometry information for the different parts extracted from the training images could be determined. The visual appearance of the local parts were matched to the codebook entries and the $p^\circ_{\omega,j}$ calculated for each visual codebook entry c_j. The distributions were assumed to be valid when matches from parts originating of at least 5% of the images were achieved. Otherwise we assumed that the respective part is either an accidental match or very rare so that a reliable object reference point occurrence distribution cannot be established. Applying these restrictions, we got 522 valid parts that were allowed to vote. From these, we took the 300 geometrically most stable clusters (see section 9.2) for our final results, as this delivered slightly superior results compared to taking all clusters.

Evaluation

For classification, we used a standard SVM with a histogram intersection kernel. The classification results are displayed in form of Receiver Operator Characteristic (ROC) curves. In a ROC curve, the true positive rate is plotted against the false positive rate for different decision values for the output of the classifier. As confidence value for the SVM based classification, we used the distance of the sample to the hyperplane. The equal error rate, i.e. the decision value for which the true positive rate is equal to the true negative rate (i.e. the classifier makes the same amount of error for the positive and negative class) can be seen as intersection with a diagonal line from (0,1) to (1,0), depicted as a red line in figure 9.9.

As a base line, we calculated global part histograms from the images, using the entire code book. As can be seen from the results in figure 9.9, the performance for the global histograms is very low, with an EER only at 60%. This indicates that the structures in all images are rather similar, and an orderless, global representation of the images is not sufficient to decide whether a bicycle is present in an image.

In the following experiments, we calculated local histograms induced by highly probable parameter combinations for the occurrence of an object. We calculated histograms from regions induced by maxima in the parameter space that were higher than 40% of the global maximum. All these histograms were classified by a SVM and and the highest decision value (the most positive distance to the SVM-hyperplane) was used as the final decision value for the occurrence of a bicycle in the respective image.

We calculated regional as well as SCP histograms using the most probable object parameter combinations. As can be seen from the results in 9.9, both local histograms improved upon the baseline. The regional histogram using the entire bounding box information and the entire visual code book performed superior compared to the SCP histogram. In the SCP histograms, only the parts with a valid object center point distribution were considered, thus a less rich codebook is available for describing the object. The SCP histograms thus have a lower complexity. Moreover, they are typically more sparse, since only the parts that agree on a parameter combination are considered. Thus they are of limited use as a sole representation of an object.

The regional histograms are able to compensate for misses of structures that could occur in the SCP histograms, e.g. in cases where the scale or object reference point estimation was inaccurate for a part. However, evaluating the false negatives of the regional histogram classification revealed that calculating a histogram for an entire region has problems with partially occluded objects and bicycles placed directly in front of very cluttered background. The wiry structure of the bicycle allows background structures to shine through the object. In these cases, the SCP histograms are superior. To combine the advantages of both approaches, we propose to append both histograms to a more rich feature vector to improve the results. And indeed, looking at the results in figure 9.9, combining regional as well as SCP histograms improved on the pure regional and pure SCP results up to 78% recall (TP rate). After that, the pure regional histograms perform better, however in an image retrieval setting, only the results for the first part of the ROC curve is important, since the user is not likely to browse all images in the database. For recall rates up to 50%, we have almost no false detections for our combined feature, thus our proposed method is very well suited for an image retrieval setting.

In figure 9.11, we show some example detections for the combined feature vector. We can verify the capability to detect and classify even difficult examples of the object class bicycles. In figure 9.10 we display some of the errors our system made. From the sample images that are false negatives, we can see that the algorithm in most cases was able to detect the right bounding box (the most probable parameter combination containing a bicycle), however the final decision value was not high enough to indeed classify this detection correctly. This indicates that the calculation of more sophisticated features on an object level can further improve the results. Our algorithm offers the perfect basis for that: since the creation of a local object descriptor has only to be performed for a limited number of parameter combinations, more expensive object models become feasible.

9.3.5 Discussion

The combination of an estimation stage to find out highly probable locations for the occurrence of an object and a bag-of-features representation based on this parameter combination has shown to be very successful.

The use of SCP histograms has advantages in cases where the object is partially occluded or background structures are intermixed with the object inside the local region. Adding the SCP

9.3 Object Classification

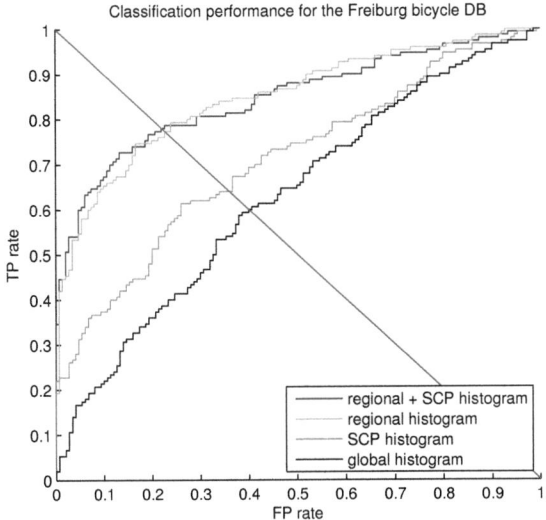

Figure 9.9: ROC curves for the classification performance of the different histogram types in comparison to a global bag-of-features approach. The intersection with the red line gives the EER.

histograms to a regional histograms can help to resolve uncertainties stemming from detections that do not belong to the object.

By using a two stage process, the use of more complex models becomes possible, that otherwise were too costly for a sliding windows approach. For example, more complex histograms involving the position of the parts inside the region and more complex distance measures to compare feature vectors might be employed. A straightforward idea is to use spatial pyramids for object representation as presented in Lazebnik et al. (2006). There, a regular grid in increasing granularity is laid over the object bounding box and the histograms calculated for each of these regions.

The output of our detector before the final decision (i.e. the most probable object bounding box and the associated regional and SCP feature vectors) can be used as an input for other state-of-the art classifiers that can also use the co-occurrence of objects in an image for their final decision by using a multi-kernel approach as presented in Lampert and Blaschko (2008). For this detector, it is necessary to have reliable features based on an object level. Our detector is very well suited for such a task.

9 Part Relations to a Reference Point

False negatives, combined regional and SCP histograms

False positives, combined regional and SCP histograms

 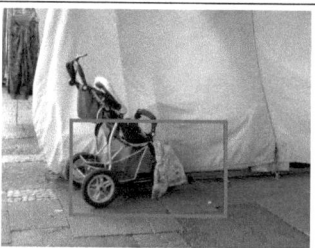

Figure 9.10: Sample false negative and false positive detections on the Freiburg bicycle database. The bounding boxes indicate the most probable location for an bicycle in the image. In the case of false negatives, the final classifier decided that the object is not present, in the case of false positives, it decided that the object is present.

9.3 *Object Classification*

True positives, combined regional and SCP histograms

Figure 9.11: Sample true positive detections on the Freiburg bicycle database.

119

10 Summary and Conclusion

Recognizing members of visual object classes in arbitrary images is a difficult task for computers. The ease with which humans are able to identify objects under varying conditions will not be met by machines soon. However, given the difficulty of the problem, significant progress has been made in this field.

Part based approaches as utilized and further developed in this work have shown to be suitable for different kinds of questions. We have looked deeply into the main components needed for part based object class recognition. As in any system where different processing stages follow each other, a final system can only be as strong as the weakest link, so paying attention to every stage is important. In the following two sections, we want to summarize our findings according to the main blocks of our part based system. We then give a small outlook how the current system can be developed further.

10.1 Identifying and Representing Parts

As discussed in the introduction, the use of local features has several advantages over global approaches, e.g. local features are less affected by global distortions, shape variability or partial occlusions. Calculating the local features from every pixel though is typically too costly. Thus, the identification of promising locations in the image has to be performed to narrow down the locations where information has to be extracted (an processed further). At this stage, no distinction between the object and the background is performed. The interest point or region detector simply identifies local structures according to some predefined criteria. An established approach is to use detectors which only concentrate on a single type of structure, as e.g., corners, blobs or edges. These points are typically very specific and might be used to establish point correspondences. A more general idea is to evaluate the change in the image signal at different scales (Loupias detector) or intensity levels (MSER detector). These detectors find a variety of image structures, but the detections are consequently less distinct. A crucial point is not to discard too much information too early. Thus, it is problematic to run detectors that only find very specific structures. Either a set of complementary detectors should be run, or a detector should be selected that finds a variety of structures, as has been shown in chapter 2.

Scale selection is a very useful property which converts point detectors into region detectors. Scale space approaches as formulated by Lindeberg have proven to be powerful and easily adaptable, as shown in section 2.2 for the extension of the Loupias interest point detector. We could

10 Summary and Conclusion

obtain superior results using our extended Loupias Laplace detector on a difficult animal categorization task proposed by the MUSCLE Network-of-Excellence.

In order to identify typical structures, the extracts from the region detectors are collected and represented as points in some feature space. This is done since the detection itself is typically not distinctive enough to precisely describe the local region. We have to rely on feature spaces that are constructed in a sensible way, i.e. the proximity of the points in the space should tell something about the visual similarity of the structures. Since these spaces are typically very high dimensional, locations in theses spaces have to be identified that are populated more densely by the samples. These areas represent structures that occur often in the images and thus can serve as prototypes for object class models. The prototypes are stored in visual codebooks. In section 4, we have shown that complicated clustering algorithms trying to recover the precise layout of the data points in the feature space are not necessary for this purpose. A simple sequential algorithm is sufficient to identify prototype parts.

To perform recognition, features that are extracted from previously unseen images are assigned to the codebook entries, by calculating the distances to the cluster representatives in the visual feature space. Here we made the observation that the part assignment function is more important than the precise partitioning algorithm for identifying parts. A weighted matching scheme seems appropriate for general features. For a sparse feature space with distinct structures belonging to the different object classes, a simple nearest neighbor matching can be superior, since it can compensate for regions in feature space that are perceptually not uniform.

The identification of the prototype parts are closely coupled to the features extracted, thus the features used should be able to identify all important visual properties of the objects under consideration.

As the term *visual* codebook indicates, only parts that are visually similar are comprised there. As shown in section 5, parts that are semantically related do not necessarily share the same appearance. Whenever we use object class models where the individual parts are treated separately, we need a way to relate semantically similar structures to another. This can be accomplished by comparing the occurrence distributions of the prototype parts on the object and using this semantic distance for a second clustering stage.

Up to this point, the individual local detections in an image are still a meaningless salmagundi, now associated with specific part labels. In order to draw conclusions, the different parts have to be set into relation. This was explored in the second part of this work.

10.2 Creating Object Class Models by Relating Parts

The simplest form of drawing conclusions from the local detections is by looking at the frequencies of the parts occurring in an image. It is a powerful representation whenever the object is prominent in an image and possesses characteristic parts. Global part histograms are well suited for representing such objects. This is especially true when the background gives additional hints concerning the objects to be classified. The basic bag-of-features approach is not able to distinguish between the object and the background. Thus whenever a histogram of the entire image is constructed, rather *image* classification instead of *object* classification is performed. In chapter 5, we have shown that for bag-of-features approaches, the performance can be improved by combining semantically similar parts, because distance calculation is typically done in a bin-by-bin fashion.

A more sophisticated way of characterizing images is to not only count the occurrences of the parts, but to additionally consider their pair-wise spatial relationship. This can be achieved by cluster co-occurrence matrices, as has been shown in chapter 8. Since the dimensionality of co-occurrence features grows quadratically with the number of parts, only few parts can be considered. Thus this approach is applicable when the images consist of simple structures (e.g. edges) and/or the detections are at a rather small scale. An example are radiographs: they are mainly characterized by bone structures, i.e. sharp edges and characteristic textures representing tissue. The simple occurrence of structures is not sufficient to classify these images, their spatial positon has to be evaluated. Our cluster co-occurrence features have shown superior performance in the challenging ImageCLEF medical image annotation competition, where exactly such images had to be classified.

The local detections can be used to determine the most probable positional parameters for an object in an image. In order to achieve this, for each codebook entry, an object reference point distribution is learned, i.e. the probabilty that an object with a certain scale is to be found at a certain direction and distance from the local detection. Accumulating these votes in an approach similar to the generalized Hough transform reveals probable object parameters. In this work, we extended the basic setting to also recover the the orientation of an object.

While the estimation of the most probable object parameters is very useful when we already know that a certain object is contained in an image, we cannot infer whether the object is indeed present from that. We thus propose to combine object parameter estimation and feature calculation. In order to focus on parts that have a high probability being related to the object, we have developed regional histograms calculated only from regions induced by the most probable parameter combinations. We additionally developed SCP histograms that are more strict: they only use parts that agree on a certain position, scale and orientation of an object, and thus are reliable features for partially occluded objects as well as object with spurious structures intermixed with the object. Experiments on a difficult bicycle database have shown that it is beneficial to combine regional as well as SCP histograms. By constructing these models only from locations with a high probability for the occurrence of the object, more expensive object models and distance measures are possible, than compared to simple sliding window approaches where a big number of locations would have to be evaluated.

10.3 Perspectives

The use of local parts for object class recognition has proven to be versatile, easy to handle and powerful. While the first half of this work – the identification an representation of local parts – is rather general, the object class models presented in the second part make simplifying assumptions about the objects to be searched for. This is necessary to tackle the complex problem. When too many parameters of a problem are evaluated at the same time, the results of the experiments are hard to interpret. For the achievement of the final goal, the detection of arbitrary objects in diverse images, more and more of these assumptions must be dropped.

An example is the identification of possible positional parameters for an object: As discussed in the introduction, an object might look completely different when viewed from the side, the front, the top or the rear. In the approach presented, single 2D views of an object are modelled. A more advanced solution would be to create a real 3D model of the object, which is inherently more complex, but can be more powerful. Specialized approaches for certain object classes exist and show enhanced possibilities compared to pure 2D techniques, e.g. for human faces (Romdhani et al., 2006). Ideas for constructing 3D models for general object recognition were explored in the master thesis of Skibbe (2008), which was supervised by the author. This work builds on techniques presented in Savarese and Fei-Fei (2007). The general idea is to learn a set of certain *canonical parts* of an object. These canonical parts are more complex entities that are comprised of smaller parts as used in our work. The canonical parts are stored in their *most frontal view*, i.e. the projection of the respective object part with the least distortion. Between pairs of different canonical parts, homographies are learned, and in this way, a 3D structure is built implicitly. Skibbe (2008) reports good results in the recognition of cars in arbitrary pose in street scenes.

In our system, all parts are related to a single object reference point, a simple yet flexible and effective technique. However, it requires that the object is rather rigid and the global layout of the parts is fixed. For some object classes, as e.g., very elongated, flexible objects like snakes, this does not hold. There the relation of parts to the object reference point is not stable, but maybe to neighboring parts or multiple points. It would be promising to explore the suitability of combining e.g. co-occurrence features and several object reference points to more complex models.

Another idea to further develop the system is concerned with the learning stage: videos are a good source of acquiring a huge amount of training data. When the objects or the camera moves, even 3D information can be captured. Motion segmentation can be used to pre-segment the data, in order to only consider object, not background features. First tests were already conducted and showed promising results.

A Notation

Symbols and general variables

Symbol	Description
$\mathbb{N}, (\mathbb{N}_0)$	Natural numbers, (including 0)
$\mathbb{R}, (\mathbb{R}_+)$	Set of (non negative) real numbers
$\mathbb{R}^D$	D-dimensional real vector space
$\mathbb{K}$	General field
χ	Some arbitrary feature space
$\mathfrak{X}$	Finite partition of a feature space χ
i	imaginary unit, $i^2 = -1$
x	Scalar value
$\mathbf{x} = (x_1, x_2, \ldots, x_N)^\top$	N dimensional column vector
$\dim(\mathbf{x})$	Dimensionality of vector $\mathbf{x}$
$\mathbf{x}^\top$	Transpose of a matrix/vector
$\|\mathbf{x}\|$	Norm of a vector
$\|\mathbf{x}\|_p$	L_p Norm of a vector
$\mathbf{M}$	Matrix
$\mathbb{1}_N$	N-dimensional identity matrix
$\det(\mathbf{M})$	Determinant of the Matrix $\mathbf{M}$
$\text{tr}(\mathbf{M})$	Trace of the Matrix $\mathbf{M}$
$\mathbf{X}$	Set
$|\mathbf{X}|$	Cardinality of set $\mathbf{X}$
$\varnothing$	Empty set
$\cup, \cap$	Union, Intersection
ϵ	Eigenvalue
ϑ	Threshold
ω_i	Class i

A Notation

$\mathcal{H}, \mathcal{M}, \mathcal{R}$	Histograms
θ	Parameter vector
ϱ	Discrete parameter vector
i, j, k, l	Discrete index variables
$f(\mathbf{x})$	Function $f : \mathbb{R}^{\dim(\mathbf{x})} \to \mathbb{R}$, evaluated at $\mathbf{x}$
$d(\mathbf{x}_1, \mathbf{x}_2)$	Distance between vectors $\mathbf{x}_1$ and $\mathbf{x}_2$
$f_x = \frac{\partial}{\partial x} f$	Partial derivative of f in x direction
$f_{xy} = \frac{\partial^2}{\partial x \partial y} f$	Second partial derivative of f in x and y direction
$*$	Convolution
$\langle .,. \rangle$	Scalar product
$\lfloor . \rfloor$	Floor function
δ	Kronecker delta function
$\vee, \wedge$	logical or, logical and
$p(x)$	Probability of x
$\hat{p}(x)$	Estimate for the probability of x
$p(x\|y)$	Conditional probability of x, depending on y
$E[X]$	Expected value of a random variable X
$H(X)$	Entropy of a random variable X
$\mathbf{A}$	Array
$\dim(\mathbf{A})$	dimensionality of Array $\mathbf{A}$
$\mathbf{A}_{\varrho} = \mathbf{A}_{\varrho_1,\dots,\varrho_{\dim(A)}}$	Content of an array cell indexed by $\varrho = (\varrho_1, \dots, \varrho_{\dim(A)})$

Special variables and functions

Symbol	Description
$\mathbf{T}$	Transformation matrix
$\mathbf{H}$	Hesse matrix
$I(\mathbf{x})$	Image intensity function, evaluated at point $\mathbf{x} = (x, y)$
$w_{a,b}$	Windowing function, centered at (a, b)
$SSD(a, b, \Delta_x, \Delta_y)$	Sum of squared differences, at location (a, b), with shift Δ_x and Δ_y
σ	Standard deviation
$G_\sigma(\mathbf{x})$	$\dim(\mathbf{x})$-dimensional isotropic Gaussian function with standard deviation σ, evaluated at $\mathbf{x}$

Symbol	Description
ψ	Mother wavelet
ϕ	Scaling function, father wavelet
$\psi_{s,u}$	Wavelet function at scale s and translation u
$\phi_{s,u}$	Scaling function at scale s and translation u
$W_s f(u)$	Wavelet transformation of signal f, at scale s and location u
$L(\mathbf{x}; t)$	Scale space representation of a signal
Lap_γ	Gamma normalized Laplacian Kernel
$\mathbf{R_M}$	Elliptical region described by the matrix $\mathbf{M}$
$HI(\mathbf{x}_1, \mathbf{x}_2)$	Histogram intersection between vectors $\mathbf{x}_1$ and $\mathbf{x}_2$
$d_M(\mathbf{x}_1, \mathbf{x}_2)$	Mahalanobis distance between vectors $\mathbf{x}_1$ and $\mathbf{x}_2$
$\text{corr}(\mathbf{x}_1, \mathbf{x}_2)$	Normalized cross correlation between vectors $\mathbf{x}_1$ and $\mathbf{x}_2$
$e_{D,j}$	Average wavelet coefficient energy, at level j and direction D
$\Theta(x)$	Heaviside or unit step function, evaluated at x
$\text{rel}_\varepsilon(x)$	Ramp function, evaluated at x
$R(\boldsymbol{\theta})$	Relational kernel function, according to parameters $\boldsymbol{\theta}$
$R(\boldsymbol{\theta})_k$	k-th output of $R(\boldsymbol{\theta})$
$F(x)$	Cumulative distribution function, evaluated at x
$\mathbf{C}$	General Codebook
$\mathbf{c}_i$	Codebook entry i, visual part i
ε	Hypershere radius
$w_{\mathbf{c}_k}(\mathbf{x})$	Weight of feature $\mathbf{x}$, with respect to cluster $\mathbf{c}_k$
$p(x, y, s \mid \mathbf{c}_k, \omega)$	Probability of the occurrence (x-position, y-position and scale s) given cluster $\mathbf{c}_k$ and class ω
$d_{\text{sem}}(\mathbf{c}_i, \mathbf{c}_j)$	Semantic distance of cluster $\mathbf{c}_i$ and $\mathbf{c}_j$
$d_{\text{corr}}(\mathcal{H}, \mathcal{R})$	Normalized cross correlation distance between histograms $\mathcal{H}$ and $\mathcal{R}$
$f_{\omega,\vartheta}(\mathbf{c}_i, \mathbf{c}_j)$	Indicating function for the semantic similarity between cluster $\mathbf{c}_i$ and $\mathbf{c}_j$, in respect to class ω, with threshold ϑ
$\mathbf{b}_n$	n-th histogram bin center
$\hat{p}^H(\mathbf{x})$	Histogram estimate for the probability of vector $\mathbf{x}$
$m(\mathbf{a})$	Label function for appearance vector $\mathbf{a}$
$\mathbf{f} = (\mathbf{a}^\top, \mathbf{o}^\top)^\top$	Local observation, consisting of an appearance vector $\mathbf{a}$, extracted at location $\mathbf{o}$

A Notation

D	Object model database
η_i	Geometry vector belonging to part i
$p_{\omega,j}^{\circ}$	Object reference point distribution of part j, in respect to class ω
$p_{\omega,j}^{\bullet}$	Part occurrence distribution of part j, in respect to class ω
$f^{\mathrm{r}}(\mathbf{o}, \boldsymbol{\theta})$	Indication function whether $\mathbf{o}$ is inside the object region induced by $\boldsymbol{\theta}$
$f^{\mathrm{p}}(\mathbf{o}, \boldsymbol{\eta})$	Function calculating the object parameters for a given geometry vector η, relative to $\mathbf{o}$
$q(\boldsymbol{\theta})$	Quantization function, which returns a discretized version of $\boldsymbol{\theta}$

B Abbreviations

CBIR	Content Based Image Retrieval
CCM	Cluster Co-occurrence Matrix
DoG	Difference of Gaussian
EBR	Edge Based Regions
EER	Equal Error Rate
EMD	Earth Movers Distance
GLOH	Gradient Location and Orientation Histogram
HSV	Hue Saturation Value
IBR	Intensity Based Regions
ISM	Implicit Shape Model
LBP	Local Binary Pattern
LoG	Laplacian of Gaussian
MBSAS	Modified Basic Sequential Algorithmic Scheme
MDL	Minimum Description Length
MSER	Maximally Stable Extremal Regions
PCA	Principal Component Analysis
RGB	Red Green Blue
SCP	Spatially Coherent Parts
SIFT	Scale Invariant Feature Transform
SSD	Sum of Squared Differences
SVM	Support Vector Machine

C Performance Measures

In this section, we define the performance measures used throughout this thesis. The basic setting is a two class problem where an entity has the label of either belonging to a specific class (being positive) or not (being negative). This ground truth has typically to be acquired manually, by labelling the data. The judgement of a classifier may or may not be the same as the true label.

Basic Entities

The basic entities used for the evaluation of a method are denoted as:

True positives:
$$TP = \text{\# of positives that were classified as positives} \quad (C.1)$$

True negatives:
$$TN = \text{\# of negatives that were classified as negatives} \quad (C.2)$$

False positives:
$$FP = \text{\# of negatives that were classified as positives} \quad (C.3)$$

False negatives:
$$FN = \text{\# of positives that were classified as negatives} \quad (C.4)$$

Based on these basic entities, the following terms are defined:

Images classified as positives (pos. predictive value):
$$AP = TP + FP \quad (C.5)$$

Images classified as negatives (neg. predictive value):
$$AN = TN + FN \quad (C.6)$$

Images belonging to the positive class (according to the ground truth):
$$P = TP + FN \quad (C.7)$$

C Performance Measures

Images belonging to the negative class (according to the ground truth):

$$N = TN + FP \tag{C.8}$$

All images:

$$A = AP + AN \tag{C.9}$$

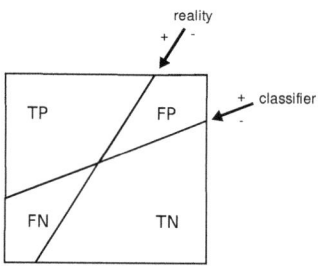

Figure C.1: Relationship of entities belonging to the positive resp. negative class and entities that are classified as being positive and negative. One partition is based on prior knowledge (ground truth), the other is performed by the classifier. In the diagram, the naming conventions for the respective combinations are shown.

Measures

The relationship of entities belonging to the positive resp. negative class and entities that are classified as being positive and negative can be seen from figure C.1. From these entities, a number of performance measures can be computed. We list them together with their alternative names.

True positive rate:

$$\begin{aligned} \text{TPrate} &= \\ \text{detection rate} &= \\ \text{recall} &= \\ \text{sensitivity} &= \frac{TP}{P} \\ &= \frac{TP}{TP+FN} \end{aligned} \tag{C.10}$$

Precision:

$$\text{precision} = \frac{TP}{AP} \tag{C.11}$$

True negative rate:
$$\begin{aligned}\text{TNrate} &= \\ \text{specifity} &= \tfrac{TN}{N} \\ &= \tfrac{TN}{TN+FP}\end{aligned} \qquad (C.12)$$

False positive rate:
$$\text{FPrate} = \frac{FP}{N} \qquad (C.13)$$

False negative rate:
$$\text{FNrate} = \frac{FN}{P} \qquad (C.14)$$

Error rate:
$$\begin{aligned}\text{ER} &= \\ \text{accuracy} &= \tfrac{TP+TN}{A}\end{aligned} \qquad (C.15)$$

Graphical Measures

ROC-Curve In order to judge the quality of a classifier for different decision values, receiver operating characteristic (ROC) curves are used frequently. For every decision value, the true positive rate is plotted against the false positive rate for differnt decision values.

In this context, the Equal Error Rate (EER) is to mention: it is the performance of the classifier when the true positive rate is the true negative rate, i.e. the same amount of errors were performed for the positive as well as the negative class.

Precision-Recall Diagram In an image retrieval setting, often the precision-recall diagrams are used. The relationship of precision and recall (i.e. the TNrate) in form of a Venn diagram can be seen from figure C.2.

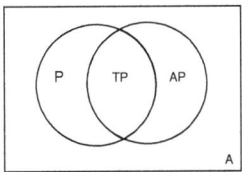

Figure C.2: Relationship of precision and recall in form of a Venn diagram. The number of true positives is set into relation to different entities. Precision = $\frac{TP}{AP}$, Recall = $\frac{TP}{R}$.

Bibliography

Agarwal, S., Awan, A., and Roth, D. (2004). Learning to detect objects in images via a sparse, part-based representation. *IEEE Transactions on Pattern Analysis and Machine Intelligence*, 26(11):1475–1490.

Agarwal, S. and Roth, D. (2002). Learning a sparse representation for object detection. In *Proceedings of the 7th European Conference on Computer Vision, ECCV 2002*.

Aksoy, S. and Haralick, R. M. (2002). Feature normalization and likelihood-based similarity measures for image retrieval. *Pattern Recognition Letters*, 22(5):563–582.

Amores, J., Sebe, N., and Radeva, P. (2005). Fast spatial pattern discovery integrating boosting with constellations of contextual descriptors. In *Proceedings of the IEEE Computer Society Conference on Computer Vision and Pattern Recognition, CVPR 2005*, volume 2, pages 769–774.

Ballard, D. (1981). Generalizing the hough transform to detect arbitrary shapes. *Pattern Recognition*, 13(2).

Bay, H., Tuytelaars, T., and Van Gool, L. (2006). SURF: Speeded Up Robust Features. In *Proceedings of the 9th European Conference on Computer Vision, ECCV 2006*.

Belongie, S., Malik, J., and Puzicha, J. (2002). Shape matching and object recognition using shape contexts. *IEEE Transactions on Pattern Analysis and Machine Intelligence*, 24(4):509–522.

Bouchard, G. and Triggs, B. (2005). Hierarchical part-based visual object categorization. In *Proceedings of the IEEE Computer Society Conference on Computer Vision and Pattern Recognition, CVPR 2005*, volume 1, pages 710–715.

Burl, M. (1997). *Recognition of Visual Object Classes*. PhD thesis, Californian Institute of Technology.

Canny, J. (1986). A computational approach to edge detection. *IEEE Transactions on Pattern Analysis and Machine Intelligence*, 8:679–714.

Corridoni, J. M., Bimbo, A. D., and Vicario, E. (1998). Image retrieval by color semantics with incomplete knowledge. *Journal of the American Society for Information Science and Technology*, 49(3):267–282.

Crandall, D., Felzenszwalb, P., and Huttenlocher, D. (2005). Spatial priors for part-based recognition using statistical models. In *Proceedings of the IEEE Computer Society Conference on Computer Vision and Pattern Recognition, CVPR 2005*, volume 1, pages 10–17.

Bibliography

Csurka, G., Dance, L., Willamowski, J., and Bray, C. (2004). Visual categorization with bags of keypoints. In *Proceedings of the 8th European Conference on Computer Vision, Wokshop on Statistical Learning in Computer Vision, ECCV 2004*, pages 59–74.

Daubechies, I. (1992). *Ten Lectures on Wavelets*. SIAM.

de Hoon, M. J. L., Imoto, S., Nolan, J., and Miyano, S. (2004). Open source clustering software. *Bioinformatics*, 20(9):1453–1454.

Deselaers, T., Hegerath, A., Keysers, D., and Ney, H. (2006). Sparse patch-histograms for object classification in cluttered images. In *Proceedings of the 28th DAGM Symposium, DAGM 2006*.

Deselaers, T., Keysers, D., and Ney, H. (2004). FIRE - flexible image retrieval engine: Image-CLEF 2004 evaluation. In *Proceedings of the Cross Language Evaluation Forum Workshop, CLEF 2004*.

Deselaers, T., Keysers, D., and Ney, H. (2005). Discriminative training for object recognition using image patches. In *Proceedings of the IEEE Computer Society Conference on Computer Vision and Pattern Recognition, CVPR 2005*, volume 2, pages 157–162.

Deselaers, T., Keysers, D., and Ney, H. (2008). Features for image retrieval: An experimental comparison. *Information Retrieval*. in press.

Donner, R., Micusik, B., Langs, G., and Bischof, H. (2007). Sparse MRF appearance models for fast anatomical structure localisation. In *Proceedings of the British Machine Vision Conference, BMVC 2007*.

Dorko, G. and Schmid, C. (2006). Maximally stable local description for scale selection. In *Proceedings of the 9th European Conference on Computer Vision, ECCV 2006*.

Duda, R. O. and Hart, P. E. (1972). Use of the Hough transformation to detect lines and curves in pictures. *Communications of the ACM*, 15(1):11–15.

Eakins, J. P. and Graham, M. E. (1999). Content-based image retrieval – a report to the JISC technology applications programme. Technical report, Institute for Image Data Research, University of Northumbria at Newcastle.

Epshtein, B. and Ullman, S. (2005). Identifying semantically equivalent object fragments. In *Proceedings of the IEEE Computer Society Conference on Computer Vision and Pattern Recognition, CVPR 2005*, volume 1, pages 2–9.

Epshtein, B. and Ullman, S. (2007). Semantic hierarchies for recognizing objects and parts. In *Proceedings of the IEEE Computer Society Conference on Computer Vision and Pattern Recognition, CVPR 2007*.

Fei-Fei, L., Fergus, R., and Perona, P. (2004). Learning generative visual models from few training examples an incremental bayesian approach tested on 101 object categories. In *Proceedings of the Workshop on Generative-Model Based Vision*.

Fei-Fei, L., Fergus, R., and Perona, P. (2006). One-shot learning of object categories. *IEEE Transactions on Pattern Analysis and Machine Intelligence*, 28(4):594–611.

Fergus, R., Perona, P., and Zisserman, A. (2003). Object class recognition by unsupervised scale-invariant learning. In *Proceedings of the IEEE Computer Society Conference on Computer Vision and Pattern Recognition, CVPR 2003*, volume 2, pages 264–27.

Fidler, S., Boben, M., and Leonardis, A. (2008). Similarity-based cross-layered hierarchical representation for object categorization. In *Proceedings of the IEEE Computer Society Conference on Computer Vision and Pattern Recognition, CVPR 2008*.

Fischler, M. and Elschlager, R. (1973). The representation and matching of pictorial structures. *IEEE Transactions on Computers*, 22(1):67–92.

Flickner, M., Sawhney, H., Niblack, W., Ashley, J., Huang, Q., Dom, B., Gorkani, M., Hafner, J., Lee, D., Petkovic, D., Steele, D., and Yanker, P. (1995). Query by image and video content: the QBIC system. *Computer*, 28(9):23–32.

Florea, F., Rogozan, A., Cornea, V., Bensrhair, A., and Darmoni, S. (2006). MedIC/CISMeF at ImageCLEF 2006: Image annotation and retrieval tasks. In *Proceedings of the Cross Language Evaluation Forum Workshop, CLEF 2006*.

Förstner, W. and Gülch, E. (1987). A fast operator for detection and precise location of distinct points, corners and centers of circular features. In *Proceedings of the Intercommission Conference on Fast Processing of Photogrammetric Data*.

Fukunaga, K. (1990). *Introduction to Statistical Pattern Recognition*. Academic Press.

Gonzales, R. and Woods, R. (1993). *Digital Image Processing*. Addison Wesley.

Gouet, V. and Boujemaa, N. (2002). About optimal use of color points of interest for content-based image retrieval. Technical Report RR-4439, INRIA.

Haasdonk, B. (2005). *Transformation Knowledge in Pattern Analysis with Kernel Methods*. PhD thesis, Albert-Ludwigs-Universität Freiburg.

Halawani, A., Teynor, A., Setia, L., Brunner, G., and Burkhardt, H. (2006). Fundamentals and applications of image retrieval: An overview. *Datenbank-Spektrum*, 18:14–23.

Hanbury, A. and Targhi, A. T. (2006). A dataset of annotated animals. In *Proceedings of the 2nd MUSCLE/ImageCLEF Workshop on Image and Video Retrieval Evaluation*.

Haralick, R. M., Shanmugam, K., and Dinstein, I. (1973). Textural features for image classification. *IEEE Transactions on Systems, Man and Cybernetics*, 3:610–621.

Harris, C. and Stephens, M. (1988). A combined corner and edge detector. In *Proceedings of The 4th Alvey Vision Conference*.

Hofstadter, D. (1986). *Metamagical themas*. Bantam Books.

Huang, J., Kumar, S. R., Mitra, M., Zhu, W.-J., and Zabih, R. (1997). Image indexing using color correlograms. In *Proceedings of the IEEE Computer Society Conference on Computer Vision and Pattern Recognition, CVPR 1997*, pages 762–768.

Jain, A. K. and Dubes, R. C. (1988). *Algorithms for clustering data*. Prentice-Hall.

Jurie, F. and Schmid, C. (2004). Scale-invariant shape features for recognition of object categories. In *Proceedings of the IEEE Computer Society Conference on Computer Vision and Pattern Recognition, CVPR 2004*, volume 2.

Jurie, F. and Triggs, B. (2005). Creating efficient codebooks for visual recognition. In *Proceedings of the 10th IEEE International Conference on Computer Vision, ICCV 2005*.

Kadir, T., Zisserman, A., and Brady, M. (2004). An affine invariant salient region detector. In *Proceedings of the 8th European Conference on Computer Vision, ECCV 2004*, pages 345–457.

Ke, Y. and Sukthankar, R. (2004). PCA-SIFT: A more distinctive representation for local image descriptors. In *Proceedings of the IEEE Computer Society Conference on Computer Vision and Pattern Recognition, CVPR 2004*.

Keller, J. M., Chen, S., and Crownover, R. M. (1989). Texture description and segmentation through fractal geometry. *Computer Vision, Graphics, and Image Processing*, 45(2):150–166.

Keysers, D., Gollan, C., and Ney, H. (2004). Classification of medical images using non-linear distortion models. In *Bildverarbeitung für die Medizin, BVM 2004*.

Kullback, S. and Leibler, R. A. (1951). On information and sufficiency. *Annals of Mathematical Statistics*, 22(1):79–86.

Lampert, C. H. and Blaschko, M. B. (2008). A multiple kernel learning approach to joint multiclass object detection. In *Proceedings of the 30th DAGM Symposium, DAGM 2008*.

Lampert, C. H., Blaschko, M. B., and Hofmann, T. (2008). Beyond sliding windows: Object localization by efficient subwindow search. In *Proceedings of the IEEE Computer Society Conference on Computer Vision and Pattern Recognition, CVPR 2008*.

Laptev, I. (2006). Improvements of object detection using boosted histograms. In *Proceedings of the British Machine Vision Conference, BMVC 2006*.

Lazebnik, S., Schmid, C., and Ponce, J. (2006). Beyond bags of features: Spatial pyramid matching for recognizing natural scene categories. In *Proceedings of the IEEE Computer Society Conference on Computer Vision and Pattern Recognition, CVPR 2006*, volume 2, pages 2169–2178.

Lehmann, T. M., Schubert, H., Keysers, D., Kohnen, M., and Wein, B. B. (2003). The IRMA code for unique classification of medical images. In *Proceedings of SPIE Medical Imaging*, pages 440–451.

Leibe, B. (2004). *Interleaved Object Categorization and Segmentation*. PhD thesis, ETH Zurich. PhD Thesis No. 15752.

Leibe, B., Leonardis, A., and Schiele, B. (2004). Combined object categorization and segmentation with an implicit shape model. In *Proceedings of the Workshop on Statistical Learning in Computer Vision*.

Leibe, B., Leonardis, A., and Schiele, B. (2008). Robust object detection with interleaved categorization and segmentation. *International Journal of Computer Vision*, 77(1-3):259–289.

Leibe, B., Mikolajczyk, K., and Schiele, B. (2006). Efficient clustering and matching for object class recognition. In *Proceedings of the British Machine Vision Conference, BMVC 2006*.

Leibe, B. and Schiele, B. (2003). Interleaved object categorization and segmentation. In *Proceedings of the British Machine Vision Conference, BMVC 2003*.

Li, J. and Wang, J. Z. (2003). Automatic linguistic indexing of pictures by a statistical modeling approach. *IEEE Transactions on Pattern Analysis and Machine Intelligence*, 25(9):1075–1088.

Linde, Y., Buzo, A., and Gray, R. (1980). An algorithm for vector quantizer design. *IEEE Transactions on Communications*, 28(1):84–95.

Lindeberg, T. (1994). *Scale-Space Theory in Computer Vision*. Kluver Academic Publishers.

Lindeberg, T. (1998). Feature detection with automatic scale selection. *International Journal of Computer Vision*, 30(2):77–116.

Lindeberg, T. (1999). *Handbook of Computer Vision and Applications*, volume 2, chapter Principles for Automatic Scale Selection, pages 239–274. Academic Press.

Loupias, E. and Sebe, N. (1999). Wavelet based salient points for image retrieval. Technical report, Laboratoire Reconnaissance de Formes et Vision, INSA Lyon.

Loupias, E., Sebe, N., Bres, S., and Jolion, J.-M. (2000). Wavelet-based salient points for image retrieval. In *Proceedings of the IEEE International Conference on Image Processing, ICIP 2000*.

Lowe, D. G. (1999). Object recognition from local scale-invariant features. In *Proceedings of the 7th IEEE International Conference on Computer Vision, ICCV 1999*, pages 1150–1157.

Lowe, D. G. (2004). Distinctive image features from scale-invariant keypoints. *International Journal of Computer Vision*, 60:91–110.

Loy, G. and Zelinsky, A. (2003). Fast radial symmetry for detecting points of interest. *IEEE Transactions on Pattern Analysis and Machine Intelligence*, 25(8):959–973.

Mahalanobis, P. C. (1936). On the generalized distance in statistics. In *Proceedings of the National Institute of Science*.

Mallat, S. (1989). A theory for multiresolution signal decomposition: The wavelet representation. *IEEE Transactions on Pattern Analysis and Machine Intelligence*, 11:674–693.

Maree, R., Geurts, P., Piater, J., and Wehenkel, L. (2005). Random subwindows for robust image classification. In *Proceedings of the IEEE Computer Society Conference on Computer Vision and Pattern Recognition, CVPR 2005*, volume 1, pages 34–40.

Matas, J., Chum, O., Urban, M., and Pajdla, T. (2002). Robust wide baseline stereo from maximally stable extremal regions. In *Proceedings of the British Machine Vision Conference, BMVC 2002*, pages 384–393.

Merriam-Webster (2003). *Collegiate Dictionary*. Merriam Webster Inc, 11th edition.

Mikolajczyk, K., Leibe, B., and Schiele, B. (2005a). Local features for object class recognition. In *Proceedings of the 10th IEEE International Conference on Computer Vision, ICCV 2005*, volume 2, pages 1792–1799.

Mikolajczyk, K., Leibe, B., and Schiele., B. (2006). Multiple object class detection with a generative model. In *Proceedings of the IEEE Computer Society Conference on Computer Vision and Pattern Recognition, CVPR 2006*.

Mikolajczyk, K. and Schmid, C. (2002). An affine invariant interest point detector. In *Proceedings of the 7th European Conference on Computer Vision, ECCV 2002*, volume 1, pages 128–142.

Mikolajczyk, K. and Schmid, C. (2004). Scale and affine invariant interest point detectors. *International Journal of Computer Vision*, 60(1):63–86.

Mikolajczyk, K. and Schmid, C. (2005). A performance evaluation of local descriptors. *IEEE Transactions on Pattern Analysis and Machine Intelligence*, 27(10):1615–1630.

Mikolajczyk, K., Tuytelaars, T., Schmid, C., Zisserman, A., Matas, J., Schaffalitzky, F., Kadir, T., and Van Gool, L. (2005b). A comparison of affine region detectors. *International Journal of Computer Vision*, 65:43–72.

Mikolajczyk, K., Zisserman, A., and Schmid, C. (2003). Shape recognition with edge-based features. In *Proceedings of the British Machine Vision Conference, BMVC 2003*.

Moravec, H. (1977). Towards automatic visual obstacle avoidance. In *Proceedings of the 5th International Joint Conference on Artificial Intelligence, IJCAI 1977*.

Müller, H., Deselaers, T., Deserno, T., Clough, P., Kim, E., and Hersh, W. (2007). Overview of the ImageCLEFmed 2006 medical retrieval and medical annotation tasks. In *Working Notes of the 7th Workshop of the Cross-Language Evaluation Forum, CLEF 2006*.

Müller, W. (2001). *Design and Implementation of a flexible Content Based Image Retrieval framework - The GNU Image Finding Tool*. PhD thesis, Universtiy of Geneva.

Nowak, E., Jurie, F., and Triggs, W. (2006). Sampling strategies for bag-of-features image classification. In *Proceedings of the 9th European Conference on Computer Vision, ECCV 2006*, pages 490–503.

Ojala, T., Pietikäinen, M., and Harwood, D. (1996). A comparative study of texture measures with classification based on feature distributions. *Pattern Recognition*, 29(1):51–59.

Ojala, T., Pietikäinen, M., and Mäenpää, T. (2000). Gray scale and rotation invariant texture classification with local binary patterns. In *Proceedings of the 7th European Conference on Computer Vision, ECCV 2002*, pages 404–420.

Ojala, T., Pietikäinen, M., and Mäenpää, T. (2002). Multiresolution gray-scale and rotation invariant texture classification with local binary patterns. *IEEE Transactions on Pattern Analysis and Machine Intelligence*, 24(7):971–987.

Ommer, B. and Buhmann, J. (2006). Learning compositional categorization models. In *Proceedings of the 9th European Conference on Computer Vision, ECCV 2006*.

Opelt, A., Pinz, A., Fussenegger, M., and Auer, P. (2006a). Generic object recognition with boosting. *IEEE Transactions on Pattern Analysis and Machine Intelligence*, 28(3):416–431.

Opelt, A., Pinz, A., and Zisserman, A. (2006b). A boundary-fragment-model for object detection. In *Proceedings of the 9th European Conference on Computer Vision, ECCV 2006*.

Papoulis, A. and Pillai, S. U. (2002). *Probability, Random Variables and Stochastic Processes*. McGraw-Hill, 4th edition.

Parzen, E. (1962). On the estimation of a probability density function and mode. *Annals of Mathematical Statistics*, 33:1065–1076.

Ponce, J., Lazebnik, S., Rothganger, F., and Schmid, C. (2004). Towards true 3D object recognition. In *Reconnaissance des Formes et Intelligence Artificielle, RFIA 2004*.

Reisert, M., Ronneberger, O., and Burkhardt, H. (2007). Holomorphic filters for object detection. In *Proceedings of the 29th DAGM Symposium, DAGM 2007*, pages 304–313.

Rodieck, R. W. (1998). *The first steps in seeing*. Sinauer Associates.

Rohr, K. (1992). Recognizing corners by fitting parametric models. *International Journal of Computer Vision*, 3:213–230.

Romdhani, S., Ho, J., Vetter, T., and Kriegman, D. J. (2006). Face recognition using 3D models: Pose and illumination. *Proceedings of the IEEE*, 94(11):1977–1999.

Romdhani, S. and Vetter, T. (2007). 3D probabilistic feature point model for object detection and recognition. In *Proceedings of the IEEE Computer Society Conference on Computer Vision and Pattern Recognition, CVPR 2007*.

Ronneberger, O. (2007). *3D Invariants for Automated Pollen Recognition*. PhD thesis, Albert-Ludwigs-Universität Freiburg.

Ronneberger, O., Wang, Q., and Burkhardt, H. (2007). 3D invariants with high robustness to local deformations for automated pollen recognition. In *Proceedings of the 29th DAGM Symposium, DAGM 2007*.

Santini, S., Gupta, A., Smeulders, A., Worring, M., and Jain, R. (2000). Content based image retrieval at the end of the early years. *IEEE Transactions on Pattern Analysis and Machine Intelligence*, 22(12):1349–1380.

Savarese, S. and Fei-Fei, L. (2007). 3D generic object categorization, localization and pose estimation. In *Proceedings of the 11th IEEE International Conference on Computer Vision, ICCV 2007*.

Schael, M. (2004). *Methoden zur Konstruktion invarianter Merkmale für die Texturanalyse*. PhD thesis, Albert-Ludwigs-Universität Freiburg.

Schael, M. and Burkhardt, H. (1998). Error detection on textures using invariant grey-scale features. In *Workshop on Texture Analysis, WTA 1998*, pages 165–179.

Schmid, C. and Mohr, R. (1997). Local grayvalue invariants for image retrieval. *IEEE Transactions on Pattern Analysis and Machine Intelligence*, 19(5):530–535.

Bibliography

Schmid, C., Mohr, R., and Bauckhage, C. (2000). Evaluation of interest point detectors. *International Journal of Computer Vision*, 37(2):151–172.

Schölkopf, B. and Smola, A. J. (2001). *Learning with Kernels - Support Vector Machines, Regularization, Optimization, and Beyond*. MIT Press.

Schulz-Mirbach, H. (1995). *Anwendung von Invarianzprinzipien zur Merkmalgewinnung in der Mustererkennung*. PhD thesis, TU Hamburg-Harburg. Reihe 10, Nr. 372, VDI-Verlag.

Sebe, N. and Lew, M. S. (2000). Wavelet based texture classification. In *Proceedings of the 15th International Conference on Pattern Recognition, ICPR 2000*.

Sebe, N., Tian, Q., Loupias, E., Lew, M. S., and Huang, T. S. (2002). Evaluation of salient point techniques. In *Proceedings of the ACM International Conference on Image and Video Retrieval, CIVR 2002*, pages 367–377.

Setia, L. and Burkhardt, H. (2006). Feature selection for automatic image annotation. In *Proceedings of the 28th DAGM Symposium, DAGM 2006*.

Setia, L., Teynor, A., Halawani, A., and Burkhardt, H. (2006a). Image classification using cluster co-occurrence matrices of local relational features. In *Proceedings of the 8th ACM SIGMM International Workshop on Multimedia Information Retrieval, MIR 2006*.

Setia, L., Teynor, A., Halawani, A., and Burkhardt, H. (2006b). Radiograph annotation using local relational features. In *Working Notes of the 7th Workshop of the Cross-Language Evaluation Forum, CLEF 2006*, Alicante, Spain.

Setia, L., Teynor, A., Halawani, A., and Burkhardt, H. (2008). Grayscale medical image annotation using local relational features. *Pattern Recognition Letters*, 29(15):2039–2045.

Siggelkow, S. (2002). *Feature Historgrams for Content-Based Image Retrieval*. PhD thesis, Albert-Ludwigs-Universität Freiburg.

Siggelkow, S. and Schael, M. (1999). Fast estimation of invariant features. In *Proceedings of the 21th DAGM Symposium, DAGM 1999*, pages 181–188.

Siggelkow, S., Schael, M., and Burkhardt, H. (2001). SIMBA - Search IMages By Appearance. In *Proceedings of the 23th DAGM Symposium, DAGM 2001*.

Skibbe, H. (2008). Detection of rigid object class instances in videos using the geometrical configuration of local image features. Master's thesis, Albert-Ludwigs-Universität Freiburg.

Stricker, M. and Orengo, M. (1995). Similarity of color images. In *SPIE Conference on Storage and Retrieval for Image and Video Databases*.

Swain, M. J. and Ballard, D. H. (1991). Color indexing. *International Journal of Computer Vision*, 7(1):11–32.

Tamura, H., Mori, S., and Yamawaki, T. (1978). Textural features corresponding to visual perception. *IEEE Transactions on Systems, Man and Cybernetics*, 8:460–473.

Teynor, A. and Burkhardt, H. (2007a). Fast codebook generation by sequential data analysis for object classification. In *Proceedings of the 3rd International Symposium on Visual Computing, ISVC 2007*.

Teynor, A. and Burkhardt, H. (2007b). Patch based localization of visual object class instances. In *Proceedings of the IAPR Conference on Machine Vision Applications, MVA 2007*.

Teynor, A. and Burkhardt, H. (2008a). Semantic grouping of visual features. In *Proceedings of the 19th International Conference on Pattern Recognition, ICPR 2008*.

Teynor, A. and Burkhardt, H. (2008b). Wavelet-based salient points with scale information for classification. In *Proceedings of the 19th International Conference on Pattern Recognition, ICPR 2008*.

Teynor, A., Müller, W., and Kowarschick, W. (2005). Compressed domain image retrieval using JPEG2000 and gaussian mixture models. In *8th International Conference on Visual Information Systems, VISUAL 2005*.

Teynor, A., Rathu, E., Setia, L., and Burkhardt, H. (2006). Properties of patch based approaches for the recognition of visual object classes. In *Proceedings of the 28th DAGM Symposium, DAGM 2006*.

Theodoridis, S. and Koutroumbas, K. (2006). *Pattern Recognition*. Academic Press, 3rd edition.

Thomas, A., Ferrari, V., Leibe, B., Tuytelaars, T., Schiele, B., and Van Gool, L. (2006). Towards multi-view object class detection. In *Proceedings of the IEEE Computer Society Conference on Computer Vision and Pattern Recognition, CVPR 2006*.

Tommasi, T., Orabona, F., and Caputo, B. (2007). CLEF2007 image annotation task: an SVM-based cue integration approach. In *Working Notes of the 8th Workshop of the Cross-Language Evaluation Forum, CLEF 2007*.

Torralba, A. (2003). Contextual priming for object detection. *International Journal of Computer Vision*, 53(2):169–191.

Turner, M. R. (1986). Texture discrimination by Gabor functions. *Biological Cybernetics*, 55(2):71–82.

Tuytelaars, T. and Van Gool, L. (2000). Wide baseline stereo matching based on local, affinely invariant regions. In *Proceedings of the British Machine Vision Conference, BMVC 2000*.

Tuytelaars, T. and Van Gool, L. (2004). Matching widely separated views based on affine invariant regions. *International Journal of Computer Vision*, 59(1):61–85.

Ullman, S., Sali, E., and Vidal-Naquet, M. (2001). A fragment based approach to object representation and classification. In *Proceedings of the 4th International Workshop on Visual Form, IWVF 2001*.

van de Waal, H. (1954). Some principles of a general classification system. In *Actes du cinquième Congres Internationale d' Estétique*.

van de Weijer, J. and Schmid, C. (2006). Coloring local feature extraction. In *Proceedings of the 9th European Conference on Computer Vision, ECCV 2006*.

Viola, P. and Jones, M. (2001). Rapid object detection using a boosted cascade of simple features. In *Proceedings of the IEEE Computer Society Conference on Computer Vision and Pattern Recognition, CVPR 2001*.

Weber, M., Welling, M., and Perona, P. (2000). Unsupervised learning of models for recognition. In *Proceedings of the 6th European Conference on Computer Vision, ECCV 2000*.

Wertheimer, M. (1923). Untersuchungen zur Lehre von der Gestalt. II. *Psychological Research*, 4(1):301–350.

Wolfson, H. J. and Rigoutsos, I. (1997). Geometric hashing: an overview. *IEEE Computational Science and Engineering*, 4(4):10–21.

Wyszecki, G. and Stiles, W. S. (1982). *Color science: concepts and methods, quantitative data and formulae*. Wiley.

Young, R. A. (1987). The Gaussian derivative model for spatial vision: I. retinal mechanisms. *Spatial Vision*, 2(4):273–293.

Die VDM Verlagsservicegesellschaft sucht für wissenschaftliche Verlage abgeschlossene und herausragende

Dissertationen, Habilitationen, Diplomarbeiten, Master Theses, Magisterarbeiten usw.

für die kostenlose Publikation als Fachbuch.

Sie verfügen über eine Arbeit, die hohen inhaltlichen und formalen Ansprüchen genügt, und haben Interesse an einer honorarvergüteten Publikation?

Dann senden Sie bitte erste Informationen über sich und Ihre Arbeit per Email an *info@vdm-vsg.de*.

Sie erhalten kurzfristig unser Feedback!

VDM Verlagsservicegesellschaft mbH
Dudweiler Landstr. 99
D - 66123 Saarbrücken
www.vdm-vsg.de

Telefon +49 681 3720 174
Fax   +49 681 3720 1749

Die VDM Verlagsservicegesellschaft mbH vertritt

Printed by Books on Demand GmbH, Norderstedt / Germany